TATTOO
Journeys on My Mind

by Tina Marie L. Lamb

© 2013 Tina Marie L. Lamb
All Rights Reserved.

No part of this publication may be reproduced, stored in a retrieval system, or transmitted, in any form or by any means, electronic, mechanical, photocopying, recording, or otherwise, without the written permission of the author.

Published by Oak Contemplations
Springfield, Massachusetts

ISBN: 978-1-7374391-0-3

Author website: www.lipstickonjenga.com
Author email: TinaMarieLamb@gmail.com

This book is printed on acid-free paper.

Printed in the United States of America

In loving memory of my Aunt Ann.

Tattoo—Journeys on My Mind
Introduction

My mother often suggested I write a book about my travels; she said I could call it *Girl on the Loose*. I'm not athletic, and I'm a bit timid so my wanderings probably won't rate as adventure. But they have kept me young at heart and open in mind. Maybe that can be shared in the telling. Intermingled with some interesting trivia and excellent fun, I've encountered unexpected opportunities to consider who and what I am. Just so you know, I'm from a working class family from a New England mill town. And with its constant prodding to conform to the local, parochial view, that mill town constantly teased me with the notion of escape. Perhaps that sensation has followed me to some extent throughout my life.

Travel does not require a lot of money. But without much of it, travel requires considerable preparation in itinerary, skills and strategy. It takes some money but with preparation and some spunk, the truth is that the world is just waiting for you to come dance. My Aunt Ann taught me to always have my suitcase packed so as not to miss any opportunities. Whenever Aunt Ann and I stepped out together, we would find a change of atmosphere. To me, this is what it's all about. I've always liked to seek out new places and I especially like to come home and reflect on where I've been. Again, I'm no athlete. The only time I was ever picked for a team is when the gym teacher forced the matter. But I have successfully hiked, biked, paddled and climbed the world over and so far, managed to return home in one piece.

While these are the journeys on my mind, they are not necessarily my favorites. If asked for my thoughts on a great vacation, I would likely suggest rafting through the Grand Canyon. If asked where I would want to revisit, that would probably be the Galapagos Islands. Why are these other journeys on my mind? With each of these experiences, there was some sort of CLICK. The world wasn't living up to my expectations or was going beyond my expectations; I recognized a new perspective; or just was reminded of an image from long ago. It's an eclectic mix of genres and places. In their own way, each left an indelible mark and reminded me that I have so much to learn. I'm not sharing my older, wiser self's reflections; it's my initial perspective that keeps these journeys on my mind. Maybe some will stay on your mind for a while too.

Table of Contents

1. Up to the Tree House 1
   A canoe trip in South Carolina, with an overnight in a tree house, was my chance to set the fun tone of tree house to right.

2. Outside My Comfort Zone 5
   Many things about traveling around southern Africa dragged me outside my comfort zone. Back home in the snow, I'm at a loss as to why I thought being at home would be so much more comforting.

3. Eye of Horus 12
   In Egypt, I didn't get to attend a religious ceremony celebrating the glory of Isis and the menus weren't written in hieroglyphics. Even though I knew this before arriving, it was still disappointing to face the reality.

4. Collecting Cow Manure 19
   Cultural empathy has it limits; something I learned the hard way in Northern India. This journey recounts the incidents leading up to the point where I lost mine.

5. Maya Moment 34
   After becoming immersed in the ruins of the Maya Civilization, I felt lucky to be able to retreat to an existent country.

6. Winter Retreat 40
   A brief winter retreat in Vermont left me better equipped to cope with the ice underfoot and planted a new perspective on my approach to life.

7. Folding Lotus Petals 45
   In Thailand, people may have looked to have far less but overall they had a lot more. I think it had something to do with folding lotus petals.

8. Looking for Tanooki 58
   When communications became muddled in Japan, locals stepped forward to help me out. It made sense that Tanooki came from that place.

9. The Howling 65
   My first dog sledding experience proved to be a lesson in team dynamics and self-empowerment.

10. Not Same 72
    Vietnam reminded me that life is not always what it seems.

11. More Than One Type of Clown 86
    A trip to see the sights around Milwaukee led me to ponder just who I am and realize I need to pick a stage name.

12. The Unexpected 90
    They have some good things going on in that land of sausage trees and elongated earlobes.

13. Covering Ground 97
    Zigzagging around Alaska helped me gain a new perspective about where I'm from and made me wonder if my hometown has a bachelors' album.

14. Honor by a Nose 114
    Southern India wasn't as hectic as my adventures in the north, but it was still unnerving in its own way.

15. Room with a Turret 131
    The Loire Valley reminded me of the dragons in my mind.

16. Desert Disappearance 138
    In western Utah, I saw evidence of wives being put out to pasture in the desert.

17. The Other Side of the World 147
    China and the USA are a lot alike except Where's Waldo seems different.

18. And the Kangaroo Danced to the Didjeridu 165
    Three weeks in Australia made quite an impression, at least the insects and the reptiles did. They were visible where they should not be and invisible where you knew they were.

19. Mushrooming Anxiety..176
    Eastern Europe provided a sideways look into gulags and accented the historical violations of people's right to liberty.

20. Cow Talk..194
    Way out west felt far away. Maybe if I had worn boots....

21. Trolls, Dwarves, and the Human Race 207
    Caving opened my eyes about what I wasn't seeing on the surface.

List of Illustrations

Tug of War..Chapter 3

Lipstick on Jenga ....Chapter 6

The Line Up ....Chapter 9

Bouquet of Giraffes ....Chapter 12

Halibut vs. Human..Chapter 13

Dragon, the European sort ....Chapter 15

Magic Square ....Chapter 17

Easy Reading...Chapter 19

Spit at Home...Chapter 20

A canoe trip in South Carolina, with an overnight in a tree house, was my chance to set the fun tone of tree house to right.

1
Up to the Tree House

My mother cut out an article from the travel section of the Sunday paper about a canoe trip in South Carolina that featured an overnight in a tree house. My memories of tree houses involved fear, scary climbs prompted by peer pressure to scale the branches beyond my comfort zone. Maybe this was my chance to revamp my notion of tree houses. On a May morning, I drove about two hours north of Charleston to rent my canoe. It was white fiberglass, a 13-foot Mohawk solo canoe, a kneeler with a tilted seat and a turkey feather stuck in the bow.

Before I set off, I asked what to do if I encountered an alligator. I was told they were not a problem. They were seen only rarely and the environment was such that they had plenty to eat. The potential for harm, I was told, hung in the wasp nests found in low overhanging bushes and a poisonous water snake that I was not likely to meet. As I was accustomed to taking precautions when canoeing on my own, I asked for a second paddle and a length of rope for tying the canoe. I was thinking five feet of rope, but I was given about twenty. While that seemed a bit much, I didn't feel right mentioning it as I had asked for something extra.

With my questions answered, I paddled my canoe on the Edisto River, the world's longest black water river and one of the three rivers making up the ACE River Basin. (ACE stands for the Ashepoo, Combahee, and

Edisto Rivers.) I pushed off into the black water. It was a weekday and I was just about the only human about. I shared the outdoor space with red songbirds, little yellow birds, great blue herons, and egrets. The air was filled with dragonflies, butterflies, and other insects. I saw a huge turtle waddle over the sand and into the water. There were lots of dead trees congregated all along the river. As I was trying to avoid one of those low, overhanging bushes that might harbor wasp nests, I ended up pushing toward a pile of dead trees and somehow my length of rope became tangled in the debris. I lost my paddle trying to untangle the rope. I was glad I had asked for a second paddle because I used that spare to catch up to the first.

 I saw a local alligator; the body length, between its big head and the beginning of its long tail, was at least three feet. It was sunning itself on the bank, but then I watched it move. Resolute in its stride, the wide, black, tire-like creature descended the sandy bank and glided into the shallow black water with me. I then began a steady stroke trying to appear like a river traveler to be reckoned with. I was reminded of the Halloween story's refrain: "The old woman said, 'I'm not afraid' and walked on a bit faster." I was relieved I didn't hit that huge beast with my paddle. What a ghastly thought!

 I had no map but was told to just follow the river. It was a winding river. I guessed incorrectly at one of the forks and found the end of a cove. No harm done as the scenery was pretty. As I paddled the 12 miles down the river, I wondered whether I would have trouble getting into the tree house. I was sunburned and my arms were shaking with fatigue. Would I have trouble climbing up to the tree house? Would I have to pull myself up with a rope? Slowly the structure came into view. To my relief, a staircase led first to a deck with a picnic table and then on up to a tree house. Inside, the tree house featured a table, chairs, a couch, and a stove. It was also equipped with playing cards, board games, magazines, popcorn, coffee, peanut butter, and lots of kerosene wicks to light. And I had gorgeous weather—hot, but breezy.

While entering the tree house was no longer a concern, I was still a bit on guard. I was warned that there were lots of copperheads and rattlesnakes in the area surrounding the tree house. The advice given me was simple enough—don't step on them. And, if bitten, stay calm so as not to speed the circulation of the venom through your blood. When I suggested that I would just make enough noise so the snakes would know to avoid me, I was told that snakes don't hear well. But, they do sense heat. So they may seem aggressive if you run before they determine your heat is bigger than a frog's. The woods were covered with a thick carpet of leaves, so keeping my eyes peeled for snakes wasn't much of a preventative. I didn't do much walking in the woods that evening. When I did venture about, I pushed a stick in front of me to disturb the layers of leaves. Late that night, I toasted marshmallows over an open fire in the woods. But it was hot, and the fire was making me hotter so that didn't last long. The bugs were buzzing outside as well. I retreated back up within the branches.

My bed in the tree house was a double futon with pillows and blankets, and nested in the loft. There was a proper ladder leading to the loft and the screened opening looked out over the river. It was beautiful. As I was admiring the view, I noticed a gray velvet spider as big as my thumb resting inside the window screen next to my head. I stared at it for a long while. It was luxurious looking but big enough to be unnerving. I looked away for a while thinking—why not share this beautiful view? When my gaze returned to the screen, the spider was gone! I wasn't sharing a bed with that huge spider if I couldn't see it. I descended from the loft and "slept" on the couch. That night had a mellow breeze, but I was on edge. The pre-trip talk of snakes included mention of a rat snake in residence at the tree house to keep it free of mice. I was assured it wouldn't bother me and that it wasn't poisonous; as such, I shouldn't be concerned if I saw it. Each time the wind rustled a piece of plastic or paper, I jumped. I shined my flashlight wherever the wind had moved something to be sure the rat snake wasn't visiting—or if it was, that it wasn't visiting too close to me. I returned to the upper loft in the morning. I shook all the bedding and couldn't find the spider, so it must have left earlier. The tree house was at the top of a hairpin curve on the water so that both ends of the loft overlooked the river. It was so beautiful. If only I didn't need to share it with the spider and the snake.

My canoe was waiting for me after breakfast. When I turned the canoe over, I discovered a black frog had been using it for a shelter. I had thought something might enjoy that sanctuary when I had turned it over the day before. So glad it was a frog and not a snake. Big water bugs were swimming around the shoreline, and I pushed off. Later that morning, I saw a snake in the water, so for all I was worth I sang "Strangers Blues" for that snake. What else could I do? I don't even know if it was a poisonous water snake; it was just a snake in the water. Spanish moss draped itself on the surrounding oak trees. Bright green geckos appeared out of nowhere. It was an adventure into Edisto River magic. But I still think of tree houses with a bit of trepidation.

> Many things about traveling around southern Africa dragged me outside my comfort zone. Back home in the snow, I'm at a loss as to why I thought being at home would be so much more comforting.

2
Outside My Comfort Zone

I am sitting in my kitchen. We are having our first snowfall, and I have lit some bees wax candles in honor of the occasion. The snowflakes are big, and the grass is almost covered. I have just returned from wandering in a world where each day the skies were a deep blue, and the sun was big and bright. I told the people I met there that I came from a place with lots of rain, where people were happy and went about smiling when the sun rises in a blue sky. They seemed to find that odd. Now I know what I told them was true. Odd is so relative. It was my return that made me realize I had been far away from home. Pulling into the Atlanta airport, a parking lot came into view, and I marveled at seeing a hundred cars all together. Culture shock! For the past four weeks, I had been wandering about southern Africa and didn't recall seeing a more odd sight. Not the man suspending a small lizard over his mouth as if to swallow it whole. Not the cave where Oryx had gathered to menstruate for generations. Not the tables loaded with scrubbed sheep heads. Not even the hundreds of dried reptiles hanging on what looked like indoor clothes lines.

I started this adventure with a township tour in South Africa. On one stop, we went to a pharmacist's shop. His grandfather was a pharmacist and his grandson will be one, but his son won't because the calling skips a generation. Dried reptiles hung on horizontal lines of rope everywhere in the shop. In addition to medicines for physical ailments, he also dealt with matters of the heart. If a girl's boyfriend leaves her for another, for example, the pharmacist will give her a potion and a rattle to use three times a day. This should cause the boyfriend to see only her when he looks at any other girl. The catch is that it only works if the jilted girlfriend is the boyfriend's first love. On this same township tour, we also visited the local bar. It was a one-room hut without windows. Inside, very low benches lined the walls. The bar is open from 6:00 a.m. to 9:00 p.m., and for 5 Rand, you could stay all day and drink. But you won't fall far if you fall off the bench. I drank white beer from the communal steel pail. The woman who made the beer told me it consisted of cornmeal and malt and took three days to ferment. (Though far from smiling, she seemed very pleased I had asked her about the beer. And I noted the male patrons seemed surprised that someone was addressing the beer maker.) The beer maker was pleasingly plump and wore a floral print turban and a striped t-shirt over a beige skirt; over her outfit was a full ruffled apron that had seen a lot of wear. After she filled a steel gallon bucket, the white beer was passed around and each patron took a sip or a gulp. It tasted malty and made my eyes burn. But maybe it went well with the barbecued sheep heads. Vendors selling sheep heads lined the streets; each table fit about 20 sheep heads set in neat rows. They said, you scrape the fur off the head and grill it.

In Zimbabwe, I took a tour called "Walk with the Pride," which was a walk with lions. These were lions born in the wild but kept in captivity. As the guide explained, this was "Vollywood" and the lions were destined to be film stars. Before setting out, we had a safety briefing. Don't have anything dangling from your body. Do not crouch, scream, or get isolated from the group. We were each given a walking stick to use to threaten any lion with the stern command "Back off!" if they became too "playful." We were told that lions pull things toward them with their sharp claws. The guide passed around a lion's claw so we could examine it. The claw was stout and sharp; it looked like it could withstand a lot of abuse. He also showed us that he was loading a rifle in case other animals, such as rhino or elephants, interfered while we were walking with the lions. Then, he instructed us not to get pumped up with adrenaline as that would interest and excite the lions.

We walked a bit in a silent line holding our walking sticks and following our guide with the rifle. Then, he stopped and we waited. After a couple of minutes, three lions and their trainer emerged from a gate about 100 feet away and walked toward us. The male, a 19-month old lion named Bunji, decided to brush up against me. This pushed me back a step. He brushed against me with only his stomach as he walked by. He had plenty of room not to sway into me, but he seemed to want me to know that I was in his territory. The other two lions were 14-month old females. The lions are fed a pile of raw meat every three days. We were told the lions swallow the meat without chewing. The guide said that when Bunji finishes his meat, he goes after the females' meat because he must think, "Hey, I'm the male here. Who are you?" One of the female lions spotted an impala and got excited, arching her long tail. She scanned the scene and determined that the impala was too far away to be worth her effort. Then, the precision hunter slunk back into her lazy-cat mode. The lions posed on tree branches after claiming the strategically placed pieces of raw meat. They posed on a pile of black rocks, where we were able to approach them and pet them once their trainer gave us permission to do so. Interestingly, their fur combs toward their head from the upper back and combs toward their tail from their lower back. Walking with the lions was well worth my being up and ready at 5:00 in the morning.

What I mostly recall of the deserts in Namibia was climbing up the crest of a tall dune to watch the sunrise and watching the sand cascade far down the sides of the dune with my every step. And, I went sand boarding down the dunes. This was just like sledding on a piece of cardboard. I engaged the full program of five descents on increasingly more challenging slopes. You lay on the piece of plasterboard so that your knees were on one end. You held your elbows up and pulled the board's front end up off the ground so that you didn't get a face full of sand. If you started turning on the way down, you simply began dragging your feet. We got a push down each hill so we would get a good start. I insisted that the guide not touch my board until I showed him my form and told him I was ready. If you touched your elbow to the surface while flying down the hill, you earned a huge burn. Trust me; I know. On the last and steepest dune, we had the option of lifting our elbows as we went over a crest to "get some air." I feared my elbow was going to scrape again just before that crest so I raised both elbows out of harm's way and flew. I was roundly congratulated for my good form!

Quad biking in and around the valleys of sand in Namibia, I had finally found a desert that looked like a desert was supposed to look. These were deserts straight from Lawrence of Arabia, vast plains and tall hills of sand. I sat in back of my driver who had been working with quad bikes for 20 years. We went way up to the pinnacle of a dune, drove around the rim and zoomed down into the valley ready to tackle another hill of sand. So glad I wasn't lost out there by myself! The wind would destroy any trace of whatever path you had already tried.

I don't think being able to recognize footprints would help because the footprints wouldn't be visible for long. On a desert walk, a San guide was telling us how everyone has a different footprint on the desert sand and that one needed to learn the footprints of everyone in one's family by the age of six. That way, if you are heading toward home and see strange footprints, you will know to approach with caution in case bandits are waiting in ambush. The San guide also told us that if two men wanted to marry the same woman, the parents would give the daughter to the first of the men to return with a tail of an oryx (antelope). Then after inspecting the animal to confirm the man who produced the tail was the successful huntsman, the parents give the daughter in marriage to that man because he had shown he was best able to provide for a new family. Hmm. He also told us that if a man kills an oryx, he cuts off the tail and brings it home to show he has made a kill and to recruit help to carry the dead beast home. Everybody feasts on the meat. After the feast, because the moon has eyes and no ears, you all dance to show the moon you are thankful for the food and, in turn, the moon will then permit you to successfully hunt another oryx. The local diet seems to be a lot like the Atkins' Diet. I was told that in Africa, the saying goes "If you can gut it, you can eat it."

And, there was wildlife. One evening at a waterhole, two Black Rhinos milled around while two lions took a drink. Another Black Rhino came with her little baby tagging along after her; it was magical watching the baby mimic its mother's every turn. On other outings, a pride of lions yawned and stretched in the shade by the side of the road; a Southern White Whale jumped completely out of the water only about 30 feet from shore; and ostrich parents walked slowly with a dozen or so chicks between them. When meeting penguins, instead of shaking hand and flipper, you tip your head alternately toward each shoulder, and the penguin will do the same. (The squirrels at home are going to have to work hard to keep up with that! But at least we can hike without a rifle.)

In Botswana, the average house was a cylindrical straw hut placed among other huts inside a square fort made of vertical bamboo poles. With the abundant termite mounds, it wouldn't make sense to live in a house made of wood. I always assume a house looks like a New England house. And, I think most locals assumed I came from a place where the houses looked like theirs. While bush camping, I was sitting on the evening ground amidst elephant dung in the midst of a group song when the local guide interrupted to ask if I had anything in my first aid bag for a scorpion bite. I didn't. I decided to swim in a river with floating hippos nearby but decided against a swim in a pond because of the fresh hippo footprint at the water's edge. I found my way in the dark to an outdoor toilet after walking dangerously close to the hippos snorting in the adjoining bushes. It was a bit like the hottest summer days at home but very different.

In Zimbabwe, I went white-water rafting on the Zambezi River. It was with much relief that I debarked from the raft. It had been a full day; my muscles were sore. But my spirit was joyful in knowing I was unscathed after having traversed the 22 rapids. Then, the guides said I may as well start my climb to the bus. I looked up; the bus was far away at the top of a ledge. After checking in disbelief that there were no steps or even an elevator, I climbed the 700 feet of steep ledge to get to the bus parked on the road. Though loath to drag out these extreme conditions, I was glad I detoured about 20 feet to reach a semi-horizontal piece of rock where I could "rest" from the steady, sharp climb. At the bus, we were treated to a free can of soda for our efforts! That night, even after all that exercise, I couldn't sleep. It was too hot. After midnight, I submerged over and over again in a filthy pool trying to cool off enough to sleep. My room had a ceiling fan, but the town's electricity had not worked for two days. I refused to melt in the heat.

Now that I'm home in the snow without threat of scorpion, I'm reading my nephew's note to ostensibly welcome me home. I'm reading: "No croc attacks on the Zambezi? Shucks. That would have been a good story about how you got your stump." If that's not comforting, what is?

> In Egypt, I didn't get to attend a religious ceremony celebrating the glory of Isis and the menus weren't written in hieroglyphics. Even though I knew this before arriving, it was still disappointing to face the reality.

3
Eye of Horus

It was inspiring to think of all the travelers over the centuries who went to Egypt to see the same sights I went to see. Sadly, I didn't get to attend a religious ceremony celebrating the glory of Isis, and the menus weren't written in hieroglyphics. I was in a country where people spoke Arabic and most practiced the religion Islam. Even though I knew this, it was still disappointing to face the reality of it. I was in Egypt during Ramadan when the fast that starts at sunrise is broken at sundown. It was an exciting time at sundown. The mosque bell chimed and people moved to eat at the ready-laden tables set at sidewalk cafes. Market stalls went dark. Even with many security guards and police on the streets, the traffic stayed crazy. Horses pulling carts cantered in the main streets while their drivers stood holding long whips, making haste to get home and eat. Or more likely, they needed a drink, as it was very hot to spend all day without a sip.

Cairo had dozens of small market stalls along the sidewalks. At a juice stall, I ordered whatever the three women in front of me had purchased, which turned out to be a "cocktail." What I received was banana pieces spiked around the rim of a glass mug that was filled with a mixture of juices from pomegranates, mangos, and papayas along with some banana slices. It was served with a fork, and I considered it a good find. As usual, I got lost here and there. A man who gave me directions to the metro one evening, even going out of his way to escort me part of the way there, told me that the Arab world is upset with the United States. I don't think I would have said anything like that to an Egyptian tourist in Boston. One evening, I was having supper at a sidewalk restaurant when a young woman selling packets of tissues approached and tried to kiss me. I pushed her away. Then, she tried to kiss my forehead, and I pushed her away again. With this second rebuff, I said, "Only with men." The men staring at the whole encounter pretended they didn't see anything.

Just about anywhere in Cairo you can see men sitting on a sidewalk smoking a *sheesha* (water bong). At a sidewalk café, I ordered a sheesha. It was smoking a green apple flavor. I was told most Egyptians favor a thick honey flavor, but that was bitter to me. My favorite part of the sheesha was its long, flexible pipe with the velvet-covered handle. It was like the pipe used by the hookah-smoking caterpillar of Alice in Wonderland. I somehow doubted the men around me thought about it that way, but maybe they were thinking about Alice in Wonderland too.

Sitting at a sidewalk cafe was a good spot to people watch. Women generally wore scarves over their heads that were pinned under the chin so that no skin below the chin showed…which might be to keep a lighter complexion. Generally, the men were of a much darker complexion. Most of the people on the street were males, who wore long, boxy dresses that reached the ground and had long sleeves. The men wore mostly light colors, and the women wore mostly black or navy. It is legal for a man to have four wives in Egypt. In my mind, this practice didn't jive with the pious fasting at Ramadan. But I found people mostly courteous and conscientious of not conducting themselves in any way that would shame their families.

After poking about Cairo for a bit, I picked up with a group tour. So glad I did. Otherwise, I would not have swum in the Nile, ridden a donkey along a mountain's edge, ridden atop a camel along a ledge up Mount Sinai, hiked the last 750 "steps" to the summit of Mount Sinai, or snorkeled in the Red Sea. And, I don't think I would have bought as much without group purchasing power. I picked the tour that included riding a donkey to the Valley of the Kings. I don't know why, but looking down onto donkey ears was charming. It was a great experience, but as I straddled my donkey, named Aliahtuht, "the ride from hell" echoed in my mind. He didn't seem partial to having a passenger. We rode up and up, and I talked to the donkey, giving him encouragement and warning of upcoming obstructions. We came upon a stretch where I had to lead the donkey rather than ride it. When I dismounted, that donkey would not budge. It was just like the stubborn donkey in a fairy tale. I had to call the guide to help me get the animal started. Ultimately, we recommenced our ascent as a team. Later, the donkey and I remained still while another pack of donkeys passed all around us coming down the hill. I think we bonded at that point. When I had to leave my fearless steed, Aliahtuht, I hoped that the short donkey would be all right on the trek back down the mountainside.

In the underground tombs of the Valley of Kings, I stretched my imagination taking in the likes of creatures with snake bodies and human legs playing tug of war. My most memorable moments in Egypt were the times I sat back apace and gazed at the huge, ancient monuments. It was like a fine chord sounding all around me. And yet it was when I got close to the monuments and looked carefully that I saw the most fantastic images. After admiring the towering Ramses temple at Abu Simbel from afar, I went inside, where pictures chiseled into the walls show Ramses chasing off enemies and consulting with gods; some gods had bird heads and some gods

Tug of War

had ram heads. At Medinat Habu, the inner temple walls pictured battles and conquests. One relief showed captive soldiers cutting off their hands and placing them in a pile to give to the victorious king. The guide explained another relief, telling us they cut the penis off each corpse of the enemy in the field to show how many enemy combatants had been slain. To my mind, South Park has nothing on those ancient artists.

At the pyramids, I sat on a camel for the souvenir photo. A man in a long tunic went off with my camera, and the camel started lopping toward the open desert. I tried to smile for the picture while shouting, "Someone get the camel!" Turns out I was atop an irate camel with an apathetic minder. But I still gave him a good tip, because he saved my life by getting me safely off that hissing camel. Olah was our guide at the pyramids and she elided the middle syllable so that it sounded like "permits." She noted that 10 years ago, visitors could climb the pyramids, but they don't allow it anymore. I was just as glad. Olah also mentioned that she had started wearing a headscarf last year and was working toward wearing full covering outdoors, because she wanted to marry a particular Moslem man who liked women to do that. And he already had three wives. I didn't say one word.

We lounged about in a *felluca* (a flat sail boat) drinking cinnamon tea. We were winding along the Nile River (the *Nilah Nee* in Arabic). There was just enough room to comfortably stretch out 12 sleeping bags on the deck. One night on deck, we danced to the Bangles song "Walk Like An Egyptian." It felt so right in spite of being in the midst of Ramadan. After lunch on the first day, I jumped in the Nile for a swim. The water was cool and clear, and the day was very hot. On the last day, I didn't swim after I saw a dead cow lying on its side in the shallow water. Still, it was with some regret that I ended the felluca and cinnamon tea phase of this journey.

We went to a Nubian home and heard about our host's engagement and the traditional three-day wedding ceremony to come. He gave us a full tour of his home and then served mango juice and guava juice. A Nubian woman drawing with henna put a swirling eye on my left hand—the Eye of Horus. Horus is a falcon, the sun god, and protector of the Pharaoh. I liked having a big black tattoo on my hand. They raised Nile crocodiles at this Nubian home. The 36-inch baby stayed in its "aquarium" and hissed at us, but I held a 12-inch baby Nile crocodile. These smaller crocs became peaceful if you turned them on their backs and rubbed their stomachs. It worked for me.

We rode to the camel market in a small truck, much like an army truck, with six people facing six others crammed onto benches that would have comfortably fit three people each. It was Friday, the Moslem Sabbath, so there was no auction. But 81-year-old Mohammed gave us a tour. He talked of fighting in World War II. He told us about camels, and we admired quite a few. I learned a camel with a big hump is a healthy camel. They then pulled a camel up front for our inspection. The camel was quite ornery, but then two boys hit it with sticks and pulled it around by its lower lip. Then, they pulled it around by its nose and upper lip. The camel groaned, and we admired its teeth. I petted his hump; its skin was rough, and its hair was coarse. When the camel sat down, each boy sat on one of the camel's knees to keep it still, but even so, the camel stood up. That scared me.

There are many donkeys in Egypt. What type? The "stronger than they look" type of donkey. Some pulled wagons with loads four times their size; I saw one of these donkeys collapse. The man riding in the wagon dismounted and hit the donkey with his fist and then with a stick until the donkey got up and continued to pull the burden. Some donkeys walked in pairs and poked at trash in the street like truants. The donkeys' braying reminded me of Pinocchio when the truant boys were turned into donkeys. Because I found the Egyptian men on the streets to be uniformly polite, I wondered if the impolite ones had been turned into donkeys.

After ordering Egyptian coffee, we were each given a coffee cup turned upside down. We were instructed to pick up our cup, smell it, and make a wish. A waiter came over to serve the coffee from a pot with a long, straight, horizontal handle. He told us that the ladies should tell him their wish if she wanted it to come true. It was a very cheeky remark for this culture, where the men and women occupy different spheres and then some.

My preparation for this trip had included a belly dancing class and our teachers had been adamant that the Egyptian style was the true dance, not like that upstart Turkish version. Upon learning that Egyptian law prohibited public belly dancing presentations, I was as perplexed as if I had arrived in Rome to find opera had been proscribed in Italy. It must have been an adjunct to my semi-dreamlike anticipation of meeting people who worshipped Isis and of struggling with the hieroglyphics on the menu. (I was relieved there truly was a sphinx.)

On my last evening back in Cairo, I was sitting at a sidewalk café. Male customers occupied all the other tables, and men waited on all the tables. I was smoking a sheesha and watching the sidewalk's activity, day-dreaming until I saw Sekhmet, the lion-headed goddess of war and healing, sitting on a nearby chair. While Horus, the falcon sun god, didn't seem all that approachable, Sekhmet seemed as if she could be chatty. Maybe it was because she wanted to know why I had the Eye of Horus tattooed on my hand.

Cultural empathy has it limits; something I learned the hard way in Northern India. This journey recounts the incidents leading up to the point where I lost mine.

4
Collecting Cow Manure

India was like another planet or maybe just another astral plane. During my first trip to India, I covered much of the northern third of the country. My plan was to make three trips to the country in order to see it all. While loathe to let much of anything disturb my arduously planned itineraries, it took me five years to calm down enough to continue my plan and return to India. I learned a lot about myself during that first trip. Looking back, it is difficult to wrap my mind around it. From the peaceful serenity of Nepal, I took an airplane flight to Varanasi. There the craziness started that pushed my state of mind and soul beyond exasperation into desperation. But I must begin my story in Nepal so you'll understand my determination to be a respectful tourist and not mock the locals. When in Rome, do as the Romans do and all that.

I read histories of India and Nepal and studied maps. But once in Nepal, I was a bit baffled by present-day cities that don't look like New York or Boston. I was there before the war (hostilities) started, and the people were incredibly gracious everywhere I went. The streets were mostly narrow and only sometimes paved. I walked around great scenes of cows resting near brightly painted yet decaying shrines. The streets were full of pedestrians, people on bicycles, bicycles pulling small, colorful carriages, Toyota Corolla-sized taxis, golf cart-sized taxis and dozens of motorbikes. And, cow dung was here and there, of course, along with goats and chickens and lots of dogs. The infrastructure left me a bit puzzled because I constantly felt as if I wasn't in a city even though I was visiting heavily populated areas. One evening, after asking for a restaurant recommendation on a street that to my tourist eyes didn't look as if it had any restaurants, I followed the proffered directions along a narrow side street and climbed a narrow flight of stairs beyond an open doorway. Upstairs, I made it understood that I was there to eat. I was led to a room with foot high tables surrounded by floor cushions, and the food was delicious. The men wore Western-style clothing, but the women wore dresses with trousers underneath or saris. I saw a parade of people that included musicians followed by an elderly man and an elderly woman, each of whom was sitting on a separate, decorated seat that was balanced on top of horizontal poles and borne by groups of men. I think the parade meant a wedding was being celebrated nearby.

I rented a van and driver to go to Chitwan National Park and was amazed at the crowds of Nubian goats I saw along the way. Whenever we stopped for the driver to get out of the van to pay the road tax, a crowd of hawkers and beggars would descend on the vehicle and bang on the windows. After a while, I started getting out with him rather than being left on my own. At the park, the elephant rides were fun, and I was told a rider's comfort level on an elephant depends on the elephant's style of walking. Some seemed to give such a smooth ride and others seemed to bounce you around in the box seat set on its back. On my rides, my general observation was none of the elephants seem to get spooked by anything they encountered. But then, they're big. And even if the elephant pulls a tree down for a snack while its transporting you, it doesn't seem to affect its gait. I had a lot of downtime between elephant treks, so I practiced the state of mellow. At an elephant lecture, we were told the elephant has 40 muscles just in its trunk and understands about 50 verbal commands. The trunk is used to fight, obtain food, and drink. An elephant can survive only two months if an accident befalls its trunk; indeed, a mouse or a spider can pose a real danger to the elephant.

I sat around evening campfires with the park staff. I generally had the choice to listen to conversations in either German or Nepalese. Considering I was in Nepal, my choice of campfire was easy. Even so, there is only so much of that I could take so I would wander to the extent possible in the gated camps. Coming upon the elephant minders, one escorted me about the elephant quarters. In the late twilight, the seven elephants seemed unperturbed by my joining them off hours, amongst the stacks of dung and bales of hay. Fires burned in various places and created a lot of smoke. In that smoky dusk, the elephants twirled and swatted the hay with their trunks before placing it in their mouths. I remember thinking that world seemed magical and deserved reverence.

Each year at Chitwan, there is a 10-day interval during which villagers can enter the National Park and cut elephant grass, pick mushrooms, and otherwise take advantage of its natural resources from which they are barred during the rest of the year. The villagers were removed from the land when the park was established in 1973. Elephant grass is wide, green grass that grows as high as eight feet tall. The villagers use elephant grass in constructing their homes, especially for the roof and to make furniture such as table tops. On a canoe ride one day, I saw people coming from everywhere, converging on the river, and wading from one bank to another with huge stacks of elephant grass. The elephant grass seemed much higher from the perspective of the canoe than it did from an elephant's back. An estimated 60,000 people were in the park that day. They cut the elephant grass with a scythe and bundled it. Generally, they bundled the elephant grass in bunches up to one-and-a-half feet in diameter and fastened the stacks using horizontal braids of the same grass. People carried the heavy stacks—sometimes triple stacks fashioned into arches leaning against their backs like a knapsack. Close up you could see that the stacks were tied on their backs with a strap that looped over their foreheads. The stacks were often larger than the people themselves such that it looked as if the haystacks were traveling about on their own. The people were mostly barefoot and had mud marks up to their knees. It reminded me of Ben Hur; it looked like a scene of multifold deprivation from a distance. I was quietly thankful that I was born on the other side of the world. As I drew closer to the people who were cutting and carrying the elephant grass, I saw they were having a great time and singing happy songs. It was both bewildering and humbling. Looks can be deceiving, and I was determined to continue my time in Nepal without rushing to judgment about what I was seeing. Less than a week later, I was on my way to India.

My journal is silent on just about everything that I remember about Northern India. Hmm. Where to start? I caught a taxi at the airport at Varanasi. After I climbed in, two men got in the front seat with the driver and two other men got in the back seat with me. The most articulate of the group explained this was the taxi's last run of the day, so everyone was being driven home in the single car. I gave them the address of my destination and the articulate one said I didn't want to go there. I insisted that I did, and he insisted he knew a good hotel for me. I repeated that I had booked my hotel, thank you, and the taxi with the five men and I drove on. We stopped at a hotel in an upper crust neighborhood. The men got out of the car and one retrieved my bag from the trunk. I sat in the taxi and told them to return my luggage to the trunk as this was not my stop. They didn't budge. The articulate one stepped up to cajole me to "just look" at this hotel; he warranted it was a good hotel. In an effort to move the standstill, I conceded. I got out of the taxi to look at the hotel, and the owner showed me a room. When I returned to the lobby, my luggage was waiting for me, and the taxi was repacked with the five men who were now waiting for their fare. I was hot and tired, and those five were draining my energy. So, I gave them their fare and expressed my irritation that I was not transported to my requested destination. In response, they swore they were helping me out and saving me from a rat hole. Arghh. With my choice made for me, I stayed at the hotel. It was adequate, and the rate was reasonable. I gave the porter a huge tip and hoped he would keep irritating people away from me. My eyes felt a slight but constant sting from the air pollution. The sensation matched my emotions perfectly. (Who were those people and how did they dare such gall?)

That evening I took a taxi to see the local temples. When I was ready to go, the taxi driver got tea and insisted I join him. There were no other taxis around, so I sat on a bench and joined him in a cup of tea. Then he insisted on taking me to a silk house, explaining that his taxi was a company car and that it was part of his agreement in using the taxi that he bring any passengers to the silk house. I was livid. In the middle of nowhere and wanting to return to my hotel, I went to the silk house. It was a building with no windows; inside was a large, empty room with only fluffy cushions for furniture. The sales people were old men dressed in white and seemed ready to empty closets of silks for my viewing. I didn't sit on the cushions or take their tea; I bought a small scarf and departed their company. Thankfully, the taxi driver was waiting, and we sped back to my hotel. He was very apologetic and I told him he had just lost himself a great tip (which he had). I felt used.

The Ganges River flows through Varanasi. It is considered sacred because it holds the karma of ancestors from the ashes of cremated corpses thrown into the river's waters. I took an early morning taxi to the Ganges River for a sunrise boat ride. The taxi driver, who assured me he could make change, somehow could not do so once we reached the river and drove off with double the fare. (Did I have a sucker sign on my forehead?) A boatman said he would take me for a one-hour ride for 60 to 70 rupees, but somehow we shook hands on 100 rupees, and in the pre-dawn, I followed him through the narrow alleys to the ghat. A ghat is a wide expanse of steps leading to a riverbank. The river was already full of bathers, clothes washers, and hawkers. The hawkers surrounded the boat shortly after I stepped into it. One put a candle in my boat and insisted I pay for it; he followed the boat for a bit in the shallow water still badgering me for payment. It became so tiresome the boatman joined in after a bit saying I should pay for it; and I told him if he wanted it, he should pay for it. The hawker finally removed the candle. It was a beautiful ride. I bought a small live fish to throw back into the river for good luck. I watched a man on another boat empty the ashes from an urn into the river. When my hour on the boat was almost complete, the boatman announced he wanted 200 rupees to let me off the boat. After a long harangue back and forth, I agreed. The Ganges was not a river in which I wanted to swim. They were burning bodies at the Manikarnika Ghat when I got off the boat. I didn't stop to watch because the boatman followed me off the boat insisting that I also give him a tip! He also wanted more money because he had given me more than a one-hour boat ride (which only transpired because he wouldn't row the boat to shore until I agreed to double the fare). Finally I gave him another 10 rupees just as another man appeared trying to daub my forehead with red dye. To my horror, I realized he had hoped to charge me for his service. Fortunately, I ducked in time and avoided the dye. Between these screamers, a young man asked if I wanted to buy a cup of tea. I implored that I had no change and just wanted to escape. He led me up a winding path to a rooftop restaurant. It was a restaurant at the hostel where I had intended to stay! To me, the lodging seemed quite adequate.

After breakfast and after my headache faded, I headed off to face the world again. I got lost in the alleys trying to find my way back to the river. The same young man who coordinated my escape helped me find the river and bought me some tea. After all of that, I decided I would go "just look" at the silk shop where he worked. We climbed another narrow path strewn with animal dung. At a colorful building on the side of the hill, we entered and went up a winding flight of steps that was narrower than the path. We stopped at a caged area and waited for a key to be lowered by a rope from above. He unlocked a sealed room, which appeared to be about 10x20 feet, that was painted in pink and had floor cushions lined up along the wall. I got comfortable, and he brought out his wares. I looked at oodles of silks: scarves, pillow covers, furniture covers, saris, artwork... This time, it was an interesting experience, and I came away carrying several purchases. From there, I wandered to the Golden Temple. After such a harrowing morning, I was relieved when the security guard returned my camera, which I had to check at the entrance.

I didn't have my hat and was getting burned by the sun, so I hailed a rickshaw (bicycle taxi), so I wouldn't have to walk the 15 minutes to my hotel. I showed him my hotel card and 10 Rupees. He agreed, and we were off. This began my three-hour trip via rickshaw. He kept pedaling fast, and I kept asking him to stop so I could get out. This rickshaw had no roof, so I had no shelter from the intense sun. After he had driven way out of town, he stopped at a clearing in the middle of nowhere, where about a dozen men were lounging about a campfire and making tea. They brought me a cup of tea, and before I left they insisted that I pay for my tea and my driver's tea. It was very inexpensive, but it infuriated me to be buying this thug driver a cup of tea. He had decided to take me to Sarnuth. I had planned to go there after dropping off my purchases and getting my hat, so at least this was a side trip on my itinerary. At Sarnuth, the ruins consisted mostly of a monastery and a shrine built in 300 BC that had been all but dismantled in 1300 AD by a Muslim conqueror. I hired an excellent guide who told me the background of each site and tried his best to sell me a sari. He said Western women liked to buy them. I told him I was a working girl and had no time for such things. When I insisted he would have to try on a sari before I would, he gave up. The rickshaw driver followed me around, determined not to lose me should a crowd show up. I can only believe it was sunstroke that led me to return to Varanasi with the same rickshaw. In my defense, I will note no other visible means of transport was available. I returned to his open cart, and he pedaled back to Varanasi. When we got to the city center, he again wouldn't stop, but kept going faster. At a square mobbed with rickshaws, I was screaming at him to stop, and he finally did. I got off the cart and gave him 150 Rupees. After all, he did pull me around by bicycle for hours even though the trip was punctuated with my loud protests. This rickshaw driver made a huge scene and drew quite a crowd (at least 100 people). Unsure of exactly what he was screaming to the crowd, I asked a nearby rickshaw driver if that driver was okay, and he said, "May I offer you a ride Madame?" I just walked away shaking and entered a building. It turned out to be the Poonan Restaurant at the Pradeep Hotel. The Shahi Tukra is a dessert that consists of two pieces of fried bread covered with creamy thin custard and crushed nuts sprinkled on top. Sometimes, a dessert can help me to calm down.

    Exhausted, still without my hat, I returned by foot to my hotel, where another marriage parade was passing by.

The horns and drums and tambourines kept the beat while the neighing horses played the melody line. Ear plugs allowed me to sleep. The next day, I wanted to send home all the souvenirs I had purchased, so that I didn't have to carry them. My 200 rupee porter offered to find me a taxi for my errand. The rickshaw driver, Ben Yogi, was excellent; so courteous and professional. He wore a white linen Indian costume and clean athletic sneakers. He took me to a tailor shop where a white-haired man, also in a white linen Indian costume, took a length of white cotton and sewed a bag for my parcel. He used a foot pedal to work the sewing machine. He wrapped string around my plastic bag of souvenirs and then pushed them in the bag he had made, securely sewing the opening by hand. I was given a pot of tea and refreshments while I waited. The refreshments were wrapped in a leaf like a lily pad and included four, folded crepes with a filling. I am ashamed to say I didn't try them. The whole lot was super gracious.

Earlier that morning, I walked to the ghats where I purchased a cup of tea presented in a red ceramic cup that looked like a little plant holder. Folks smash them to the ground when they are finished with the tea. I suppose that way they'll know they're getting a clean cup with the next beverage. Rickshaw wallah Ben Yogi said that people smash the tea cups because they were cheap, costing only 8 rupee for 40 cups. I drank my tea while chatting with a young man about the cricket practice going on around us. It felt so peaceful. They even invited me to play. I just couldn't smash the ceramic tea cup, so I carried it around with me as I continued my day. The mug finally broke when I fell in the slippery, sinking mud near the Manikarnika Ghat. Two workers helped me up and showed me the fastest route to the river to wash my mud-covered hands. So, I washed my hands in the Ganges River. When I returned from the river, another man beckoned me to follow him to a balcony with a wonderful view of the funeral pyres. I watched a shaven man in white set afire all five sides of a clothed body laid out on a stretcher covered with wood. The man standing with me on the balcony shared some interesting information. No Indian women were permitted near the pyre area or balcony because five years earlier a woman was thrown on her husband's burning corpse. The government subsequently became very strict on regulating the comings and goings in the area. The eternal flame used to light the corpses is said to have been kept burning for 5,000 years. Not every corpse is burned such that their ashes can be dispersed in the Ganges. Those considered impure (which include children, pregnant women, and those who die from a snake bite) are buried instead. Holy men are buried too because they go straight to Nirvana rather than being reincarnated. He also pointed out that the son and male onlookers (remember, female kinfolk were not allowed to attend) weren't crying at the funeral pyre because the deceased was starting his next life. The shaven man was the oldest or youngest son of the deceased. He shaved his head and stayed in the same clothing and in solitude for 12 days after the father's death to conduct the funeral rites. After voluntarily imparting this information, the man standing with me on the balcony asked for payment for his conversation!

Cow manure is collected for fuel to keep home fires burning. I saw it all around—particularly set out on a roof or some other flat area to dry in the hot sun. The women did this work all dressed up in beautiful saris and covered with gold jewelry. They looked as though they were ready to leave for the ball, but instead they walked toward a field, picked up cow dung with their bare hands, placed it in a basket, and finally carried the basket full of cow dung on their heads for the return trip. When they arrived at home, they would remove the cow flaps and flatten them with their hands into round, flat shapes. Once the manure was properly shaped, they would lay the pieces out to dry. (If I ever thought I didn't like my job, I was wrong; I like my job very much.) Women seemed to do the least desirable work in India. Riding along a paved road one day, I saw women decked out in colorful long dresses and gold nose rings working on road construction using implements that looked more appropriate for a flower garden. The insufficient tools made the work far more physically demanding than we are accustomed to seeing in road construction in the U.S.A. I saw these working conditions as just another indicator of women's status there.

A story in the *Hindu Times* said a businessman had three wives burn to death in seven years. The editorial page cartoon was captioned: "We'll find the right woman for you even if we have to burn a few more." Officials estimate that about 4,000 such murders are committed each year. They say dowry deaths are reported as kitchen fires; that is, if they are reported at all. Officially, dowry is prohibited. These murders are common if a groom's attempted extortion of the wife's family fails. Generally, this fire starts once a wife is induced to light a match in a petrol-strewn room. The *Times of India* reported that in the State of Orissa, a group of approximately 20 villagers had murdered a woman along with her whole family because of the woman's criminal conviction. Earlier, the wife had been convicted of sorcery and was fined 2,000 rupees. Then someone in the village became sick and that person, along with others, blamed the convicted sorcerer, burning down her house at night while she and her family slept. I read other articles of violence against women. Other women perpetrated much of this violence against women. For example, the news stories indicated that the mother-in-law was frequently responsible for a wife being burned to death when the wife's family fell short on dowry payments. I guess that's the way of the world…relying on members of the oppressed group to act as the oppressor.

I was scheduled to visit the sister of a family friend in Delhi and even stay over on a Friday night. This was a big mistake. The sister was gone for the weekend, but I met her husband, son, brother, butler, and two men her husband employed. One of the employees picked me up at the airport and brought me to my hostess' home. As soon as I arrived, I felt trapped. The minor nuances and unspoken pressures I felt go far beyond any words I can express. So there I was in India passing the time by reading an American paperback novel I found around the house. Suffice it to say that this is very unlike me. After spending hours with the son and butler, the husband arrived with a business companion at midnight and sat down to supper. I was acknowledged, sympathized with, and cajoled into tasting sickeningly sweet foods that I knew I shouldn't taste at that hour. The highlight was when he insisted on telephoning my father to tell him I was safe. My mother answered the phone, and upon demand, she put my father on the phone. My father listened to the accent for a minute before asking him to hold on because his wife would be the one who would talk with him. I still remember how fortifying I found that snubbed look on the face of my conceited host when my father refused to converse with him. I would like to report that things got better from there, but they grew worse.

At dawn, within three to four hours of the sickeningly sweet foods, I became very sick. When I tried to call for a taxi to get to a pharmacy, my host insisted that I let him provide transportation. An hour later, I was traveling in a big car with two goons who worked for my host. We stopped at a hospital, which I was told had a pharmacy. I found the pharmacy and obtained the pills I needed. Then I learned my host had arranged for me to see his surgeon. Under escort, I saw the surgeon and somehow found myself agreeing to stay in the hospital for intravenous hydration until the evening. So beginning at 11 a.m., I stretched out on a bed hooked up to an intravenous tube dripping glucose with two goons posted outside my door. I watched a cockroach prowl around my tray table. Later, when I was cleaning up my tray, one of the goons said, "Don't do that. Why do something when you can pay someone else to do it?" (Coming from New England, that comment sealed my already poor impression of him.) At 4:15 p.m., I was told I would have to stay two nights. Apparently, no discharge staff was available until Monday morning; recall this was a Friday afternoon. I learned all this from the two goons stationed with me in the hospital. If that wasn't news enough to enrage me, I didn't need to wait long for more. One of the goons, the host's personal secretary, gave the hospital his approval to give me a series of intravenous antibiotics! This was after I had made it clear I would not consent to any such treatment. May he be reincarnated as a suburban mouse to be eradicated properly. Thankfully, it was toward the end of the glucose injection that I had asked to be disconnected from the intravenous tube so I could use the bathroom. When I returned to the bed, without any notice to me, I saw that the intravenous tube was now attached to a full bottle of medicine rather than the glucose remains. I got into bed. The nurse eventually entered and even tried to connect me to the intravenous tube while I clearly instructed I would not condone any antibiotic injection into my body. My words fell on deaf ears. Unbelievably, I engaged in a physical struggle with the nurse to stop her from starting the antibiotics. (I was even charged for the open antibiotic serum that I had expressly declined.) Fortunately, the brother of my absent hostess was visiting, and by playing out a soap opera with me in the hospital, he managed to get me discharged. When I returned to my host's home to collect my bags, the son wanted to know if his family was letting me leave. Clearly, they had gone through my luggage while I was at the hospital, maybe looking for contact information. But I was lucid so they could have just asked me. I swear the household seemed willing to kidnap me if the husband said I was to stay. The brother of my missing hostess, acting on my behalf, had a long conversation with the husband. Ultimately, I escaped. Even the brother didn't want to leave me at my hotel when he learned that the guide for my upcoming tour hadn't yet checked in. After another confrontation, he let me go. I understood his bravado had helped to free me so I don't know. (It seemed the brother was doing the honorable thing to extricate me, but his outward condoning of the husband's behavior remained a great obstacle to my considering him to be an honorable man.) Calling it an unfortunate situation is just too kind. I ultimately checked in at the hotel. After a long shower, I paced back and forth in anger for the rest of the night. And, I noticed the goons lurking around the hotel lobby the next day. Days later, I was still having nightmares about those people.

The frustration abated but also continued. I went to the hotel lobby to get my hotel key because you were asked to leave your key at the desk when leaving the room. I called for the hotel staff's attention and one of the all-male crew even nodded in my direction. I waited for a bit assuming they were busy with a situation that had come up unexpectedly. Well, then a man came in behind me, and all five of the men on the other side the counter jumped over to greet him, asking if they could get a room key for him. He was an Englishman and noted that I had been waiting first. I thanked him as we got on the elevator. If this man hadn't appeared, who knows how much longer I would have waited before being able to access my paid room. I think it was at that point that I decided to be ruthless with personal inquiries and taking what was due to me. I had tried cultural empathy and would leave any more of that to my betters. I'm not asking you; I'm telling you.

Even with that attitude, my 3-week tour of Rajasthan, the largest State in India, was great, with puppet shows and camel safaris and rat temples and painted elephants and cobras dancing up from wicker baskets. Everywhere, cows and goats were all around everything. One interesting bit was being chased down a narrow path by a big white cow that was foaming at the mouth. I ducked into a building and shut the door. I had barged in on a family at supper, and the woman of the house got up and managed to get the cow off of her stoop with a soothing voice and by wrapping her arms around its head to move it away. Once I said my thanks, I bolted to get away from that cow. After my tour, I returned to Delhi and doubled my pace to take in the sites I had missed while reading the American paperback novel. "I enjoyed my trip with so many turbans and saris and nose rings, and there were people all around all of the time." This is indeed what my journal says, but this isn't the journey on my mind. If I had not been there, I wouldn't believe it. Once home, it took me a full two weeks until I was comfortable being civil rather than belligerent. When I recounted some of my experiences, people suggested I was treated with such disregard (when I wasn't being studiously ignored) because I am female. I tried to look at it that way, but in the moment, I had no doubt it was a personal affront. I'm not sure I was wrong. Either way, it wasn't good. I did come back, however, seeing life differently in some ways. It is probably because of this time in India that I was saddened when Massachusetts outlawed Uzis. But the part about the soldier with the rifle on duty at a historical site wanting me to give him more and more money will have to wait for another day.

After becoming immersed in the ruins of the Maya civilization, I felt lucky to be able to retreat to an existent country.

5
Maya Moment

After extensive reading and a semester course on the Maya Empire, I decided to take a trip to see Maya ruins. I had learned enough to muddle through their text and understood a bit about the rulers' bloodletting to communicate with the gods. If the howler monkeys I encountered my first night were there at the time of the Maya Empire, I bet their loud snoring noises didn't let the rulers have a restful sleep. Maybe that accounts for those bloodletting rituals. Lack of sleep could make anyone desperate to speak to those gods about rectifying the matter.

Just as Bohemia no longer exists, there is no Land of the Maya anymore. Plotting my course, I started out in Belize which used to be part of Guatemala until the British claimed it as a colony in the 1700s. As a former British colony, the population speaks English. The border between Guatemala and Belize was formalized in the 1950s. I learned the Belize national anthem (circa 1950) starts:

"Oh land of the free by the Carib Sea
Our manhood we pledge to thy liberty
No tyrants here linger, despots must flee
This tranquil haven of democracy."*

In the local newspapers, I read that Belize had offered a passport to any Hong Kong resident—for $50,000 during the mass exodus before China's take over. While 300,000 people bought a passport, the government could only account for money from about 600. The immigration minister was blind, and said he just signed papers as his staff presented them to him. Other Chinese had settled in Belize earlier in the 1800s. I saw a sugar refinery, for example, built in 1865 by Chinese and Barbados citizens. It was closed just three years later in 1868. Now, a tree was growing around the structure and a three-inch bat was hanging on the inside wall. I also saw a line of trucks packed with large sticks waiting to get into a newer sugar refinery. The sticks were sugar cane (which can stay cut for more than three years before spoiling). The refinery burns the sticks themselves, but the sucrose (sap) keeps the sugar from burning.

The Maya also had settled in the land now called Belize as the country is home to some Maya ruins. Near the Lamanai (crocodile) ruins, the local people burned the first Christian church, which was built by the Spanish. On that spot, the locals erected a stele. A stele is an upright slab of stone relief, much like a large, rectangular grave marker. Under the stele, they buried a 15x15 inch carving of a crocodile head; the crocodile's mouth was open and a person's head sprouting deer antlers was peering out. If I understood correctly, this carving represented a god looking out of the crocodile's head and the god took the form of a crocodile from time to time. Undaunted and intent on colonizing the location, the Spanish rebuilt the church. Nearby were strangler fig trees choking larger trees, a metaphor for this colonization.

The cave at Che Chem Ha was found while a man was collecting fig palm leaves for roofing in 1989. His dogs chased a rodent under a rock, and when he kicked away the rock, he found the cave. I took a tour of this cave that the Maya had abandoned by 900 A.D. I was about the most physically fit person on this tour. Our guide was very tactful. He stopped to identify plants in the lush forest along the steadily uphill trek to the cave, giving us couch potatoes time to catch our breath. Three dogs stood watch for us at the cave entrance while we humans went in. With the high elevation, it was warm and humid inside the cave. We rappelled down a slope under an overhang and gathered in a room with a high ceiling. In the center was a six-foot diameter circle of stones with an erect stone about two feet high in the middle. They had been unmoved since the 1989 discovery. We then climbed a wooden ladder onto a ledge to see 36-inch wide pots that looked like black caldrons and dated from 200 B.C. One had a brown sandy substance in it that the guide described as dry corn. Another had been turned over, and its bottom smashed to release the spirit! This cave had been used for religious purposes so that the sun and moon would continue to rise and shine each day and night. When we left the cave, the three dogs were waiting for us.

Fearful of the violent fates endured by some western tourists in prior years and knowing the roads were not made for quick escapes, I signed on to an organized tour to cross into Guatemala to see more Maya ruins. In 1696, the Spaniards won the final battle against the last Meso-American, non-colonized people in Guatemala. So the violence isn't new there. We stopped at the site of the battle, and I took a photo of a dugout canoe. (I saw dozens of unpainted, dugout canoes. I asked a taxi driver if a shop made them, or if you needed to make your own. You needed to make your own.) Guatemala gained its independence from Spain in 1821. A total of 22 languages are spoken in Guatemala, and few learned Spanish as a way to resist the "conquerors." The Coca Cola cans were labeled in Spanish. So did the Spaniards win the war as well as the final battle?

I think the tour companies won the final battle. I had studied Maya history and art and writing and was all set to see the sites when the newspapers reported a bus being hijacked. It was a school trip and the bus was filled with female students and a few nuns serving as chaperones. The girls were all raped and the nuns were all killed. I decided to visit alternative destinations but continued to read books on the Maya until finally... I don't generally consider it a good use of my vacation time to go on an all-inclusive tour. But there I was in Guatemala where each of my pre-paid meals was served with bread and butter and nothing like what you might expect in Latin America. As I was enjoying the tranquility of my safari lodge, I noticed in the distance, a worker had slashed his hand. Nobody seemed to be around to help him so I grabbed my first aid kit and ran over to him. After I cleaned and bandaged his cut, we spent some time conversing and later in the day, he brought me some chicken and rice. It left me disconcerted; it was much simpler when I was certain I should avoid rather than engage the unknown. What was this package tour saying about my views on human nature or about my nature? I continued on, but less blissfully.

Cahal Pech means "place of the ticks," so named by archeologists traversing the fields to the ruins and encountering numerous ticks every day. I didn't see any ticks, but there were plenty of mosquitoes. The Maya cities are thought to have been abandoned by 850 A.D. due to social, political, and economic disorder. My favorite ruins were the huge masks set in stone relief. These stone faces were bigger than my complete body, head to toe. Were they the heads of giants who had turned to stone? Were they doomed to bear witness? Were they genies waiting for someone to rub their lamp? I suppose every culture has its giants and castles.

At Tikal, I shook with fear walking up the temple steps. The goal was to watch the sunset from the top and then get back down to the ground before dark. To add to my frustration with my timidity, a young man passed me trotting along like the steps weren't tall, uneven, and crumbly. A Spanish team was spending one million dollars there to dig out a building called Temple V, which was built circa 150 B.C. Eighty percent of the buildings at Tikal have not been excavated. The Maya built structures symmetrically so you can guess what the other side of the lot looks like if you uncover the first. I'm told archeologists prefer to unearth different types of buildings rather than repeat structures. Tikal was settled in 600 B.C. and had a population of at least 200,000 in its heyday. Did they even dream someone like me would climb the temple steps? I hear they used a lot of opium for the religious rites, so who knows what visions they had.

There were many steles at Tikal. One stele from 771 A.D. showed the 29th and last ruler of the Jaguar Dynasty. He wore an elaborate headdress with ear flares (fluted cylinders hanging from his ears past the headdress) to help him hear well. I could understand why he was the Dynasty's last ruler; he had that Louis XVI, over-the-top look. These steles were taller than I was and were originally painted red. The Teotechuan people introduced human sacrifice to the Maya in this part of the Petan (the northernmost Department in Guatemala) when they conquered Tikal. Decorating the sacrificial tablets (short stone cylinders, about 18 inches high and 4 feet in diameter, which were placed in front of each stele) were carvings of unfortunate people ready to be "sacrificed." Were they volunteers? Did they win the lottery? Were they unable to pay their debts? The word is they were "captives." These captives were bound sort of semi-scrunched on their backs, and then their hearts were removed. The blood was collected and smeared on the altar. After a day, the bodies were cleared and burned but the blood remained. Much incense was burned to cope with the stench. Bath houses were located outside the temple area. You needed to bathe before entering the temple area for the bloody ceremony. (That comes naturally).

I recall being quite put out that afternoon after having pondered those sacrificial tablets. Here were public altars for placing bound captives so they could be ceremoniously butchered; it was not something I would put in the nonfiction section. But here it was, or so it had been. It made me think. I know there has been and continues to be condoned murder worldwide. (You would think the famous murals showing the captives' finger nails had been removed would have prepared me.) But having public altars for ceremonially removing their heart with s spoon was beyond the Sheriff of Nottingham even. It reaffirmed my belief in the slippery slope notion. At home, we now publicly jail people for years without charges, let alone indictment. Prisoners are tortured. Is there no limit to what people will tolerate as acceptable? As I knew I would, I calmed down about tolerating the unacceptable. After seeing these altars for slaughter, though, how did I do it? I did it with a generous helping of coconut ice cream after a wonderful local dinner. *Ochote* is a red dye used in cooking by the Maya. It gave the chicken a slightly sweet and sour taste. By the next morning, I was pondering the many sorts of birds in the land of the Maya. Maybe a moment of horror is all we mortals can handle.

---

*Land of the Free (1963) is the national anthem of Belize. Words by Samuel Alfred Haynes and music by Selwyn Walford Young.

A brief winter retreat in Vermont left me better equipped to cope with the ice underfoot and planted a new perspective on my approach to life.

6
Winter Retreat

I was retreating north. After having driven for hours on Route 93, I kept seeing signs for Canada and warnings that Route 93 was ending. It was a bit nerve-wracking because I was aiming for the intersection of Route 93 and Route 91. How could one be ending before it intersected with the other? After that quandary was sorted out, I was soon off the highways all together. It was dark, but thankfully the fog had lifted. I was on my way to a cabin that would be on the right-hand side of the road. The directions said one car could fit in front of the cabin, and two clearings beyond the cabin would fit two cars each. The icy dirt road wound around and up and down. I got to the magic 0.8 mile mark of which my directions spoke and saw nothing. Then I passed three cars squeezed together off the road on my right. That couldn't be it. I saw no cabin, and I was going to a cabin with space for only one car in front. A quarter of a mile later, I saw two cars had pulled off the road in an area that had been plowed. Were these campers or hikers still in the woods who had parked at a trailhead? When I came to another pair of cars parked off the road, I figured that the first cars must have been parked in front of my destination. After a time, I came to a spot with enough room to turn around, and back I went. When I arrived at my purported destination and emptied my gear from the trunk, I couldn't leave to find a parking space until I was sure a cabin was somewhere in the vicinity. I hollered out at the trees. Why do I do these things? Then, I got out my car flashlight and began walking into the woods. Beyond the cars was an ice trail in the snow. It even had narrow bridges. At about 100 feet in, I saw someone with a light in the distance and hollered out: "Are you at the winter retreat?" She yelled back her answer: "Yes!" I yelled that I would be back after I parked my car. Back at my car, I set off. This was a narrow road. Three cars were jammed into a space that I understood as being described as a space for one car. I tried parking in one of the other places that was plowed out. There was no way in hell that either of the two parking places beyond the cabin would fit another car. Despite being intermittently stuck in the deep snow, I drove on. The next plowed-out place was some minutes away, and nine-tenths of a mile from the clearing that led to the cabin. I turned around and drove past the cabin in the other direction. Six-tenths of a mile later, I found another clearing. I parked and headed off on foot up the hills of ice. It was very dark and not a starry night. I was hoping the batteries in my car flashlight would hold out. I couldn't remember the last time seeing it, let alone using it. My headlamp was packed with my gear, which sat on a mound of snow near the cabin clearing. I was hoping I didn't meet any frightened—or frightening—animals. I was nearly overwhelmed with the darkness and the ice and the uncertainty of where I was or where the cabin would turn out to be. Finally, I got to the clearing populated by the three cars and my gear. Still with the car flashlight, I collected my gear and headed off to the trail where I had heard someone say "yes" about this being a winter retreat. I found the cabin. I recall being greeted by the organizer, who seemed impressed that I had carried all my gear in one trip to the cabin. (I was pleased, too, because she seemed like an outdoorsy athlete. All that foreign travel on a shoestring had taught me how to run up and down stairs to catch a train lugging all my belongings without dropping them. I do have *some* skills). I entered the cabin warmed by a woodstove and sat down to a Bohemian meal; you know the kind with the homemade soup and multi-grain loaves and the pesto and all the fixings. It all seemed very fitting for a retreat, and I was feeling victorious.

On Day Two, I participated in a writing workshop. We each took a "writing prompt" among varied strips of paper, like fortunes already removed from the fortune cookies, piled in a cereal bowl. After we each obtained a prompt, we were told to write. That's all. Some people came up with awesome poetry or metaphysical metaphors and one writer prepared a stoic reflection on animal tracks. I guess I should have asked some questions about the purpose of the writing prompt. The writing prompt I pulled out of the bowl read: "The bird was making her nest with a…"

So I wrote: "The bird was making her nest with a shred of cloth that had been recently attached to my laundry hanging on the clothesline. My sister used to borrow my new clothes. My mother would throw out my old clothes. And now this bird is appropriating my clean clothes. The bird was making her nest with a lot of gall if you ask me. Specifically, she took one of the knots on the edge of my belly dancing skirt. Does she hope her babies will grow up to be belly dancers? I kind of like the idea of birds belly dancing for the worms. It would probably annoy the cat though. The bird was making her nest with an air of innocence, but I think she knew exactly what she was doing. The other birds are chirping like they think so too. I can't tell what the cat thinks. Cats are so hard to read. The bird was making her nest with a dexterity that seemed out of place for such a short beak. I pull the cord to my hood with my teeth sometimes, and it's not easy. I don't think I could play *Jenga* with my mouth. That would take too much whiskey to even try. I wonder if the bird feasted on some inebriating berry before she started to make her nest with her beak. The bird was making her nest with a pioneer determination and know-how that I feel sure I lack and with a tassel from my skirt that I know I now lack. Good for her. I'm going to follow the cat's lead and take a long bath followed by a longer nap. At least I got to see the bird making her nest."

On Day Three, we hiked for hours stopping intermittently to remove our sketch books from our packs and then stay quiet in our chosen snow patch and sketch the winter tree buds and the animal paw prints. A tree trunk reminiscent of the android R2D2 kept vigil in the snowy forest. (Perhaps it was truly an android in awesome camouflage.) Back in the dry cabin, where the floor was heavenly devoid of ice, we 12 participants shared our reflections on the retreat. I had sat in the snow and sketched winter plant life; I had used water paints to interpret the various winter vistas from the cabin porch. (Whenever I look at trees nowadays, I note whether the branches are symmetrical or not.) But I had just about had it with the lack of comfy furniture, the many layers of clothing, the urinating in the snowy woods, the struggle to remove my mitten to use my gloved hand to get a dry tissue for my wet nose. Yet, this is the journey on which I found YakTrax (ice crampons that go on easily and stay on securely until you decide to take them off). Maybe I'm still not a fearless winter warrior, but I'm a lot less timid now. As I drove away, I was thinking, "The bird is flying south..."

Lipstick on Jenga

> In Thailand, people may have looked to have far less but overall they had a lot more. I think it had something to do with folding lotus petals.

7
Folding Lotus Petals

Noy met me at the airport and drove me to a lovely guesthouse with spacious gardens. My room wasn't ready but they gave me a guest room to let me freshen up. Coming out of the shower, I saw my luggage was no longer about, but a floral sarong had been laid out for my use. Men's sarongs go to the knee and have checks or stripes; the checkered sarongs resemble tablecloths. Women's go to the ankle and generally have floral patterns. My sarong is five feet of material that I have wrapped around me like a tube; some buttons would have helped. (I want my jeans and t-shirt.) I have been awake for most of the last 36 hours and everything is moving very fast and all is hot. I just returned from a ride in a *hong yao* (long boat) to downtown Bangkok, passing rocket boats (long, colorful, and narrow motor boats that go 60 mph); a Buddha shrine with a dragon at its base; and bank boats that brought banking to homes. We passed rice barges, large, wide boats that transported bags of rice and served as family residences. We passed red-shirted navy practicing their rowing using oars tipped in gold to row royal barges with golden dragon heads at the bow. This was the scene at the start of my first day of my first visit to Thailand.

With the intense sun bearing down on our open boat and then clamoring up a ladder to a loft restaurant and then climbing down that same ladder after lunch, I was feeling nauseous as I settled back into the boat. (It felt like I was overdue to get out of the sauna, but that was not an option.) It is the beginning of the dry season here. Waters are 45 inches higher than usual, and houses, at times, are so flooded that the people need to flee to the second story. We were in a bit of a rush to return from our boat ride before the ocean high tide increased the river height, which would make maneuvering under the bridges impossible. I was relieved that the boy wearing feminine white sandals and red nail polish helped us with our boat departure; I know I wasn't being much help. My sense of wonder was magnified by my horror at the intensity of the hot sun. My sarong was feeling like my favorite jeans by then.

But the sensation of being bombarded by the sights continued. There was too much to take in to get comfortable. A huge 150-foot dragon reposed in front of a shopping mall. On television, I watched the Flintstones dubbed in Thai. At the markets, carts offered three frogs roasted on a stick; the frogs were salt-dried and then roasted. Buckets of water were heaped full with live frogs wearing yellow bands about their middles. When I stopped at a vendor's cart for an orange soda, the vendor took the bottle and opened it. But before she would take my money, she scooped crushed ice from a cooler into a clear plastic bag, poured the soda into the bag, twisted the bag closed, and stuck in a straw; she gave me a bag of iced soda. At another market, a cockfight was in progress in a sunken area, much like a children's pool with about a six-foot circumference. One rooster was twisting his neck around the other rooster's neck. A crowd of men was cheering them on. Roosters crowed constantly wherever I travelled in Thailand.

Bangkok teamed with people and crazy traffic. After completing some errands, I took a *tuk-tuk* ride back to my hotel. The tuk-tuk is small open jeep-taxi, and this one had a canopied roof. We rode on a six-lane highway with three lanes in either direction and no dividers. It was like an amusement park ride. Cars cut us off. We cut off other vehicles. I held on for dear life as we went around sharp corners. At the airport in Bangkok, a van driver pushed double-parked cars out of the way so we could leave. He explained that people leave their cars parked in neutral gear in order to accommodate this practice. Sometimes they might find their cars 50 feet away from where they parked because the cars have been pushed so many times. At the time of my visit, an estimated ten million people lived in Bangkok, and there were three million cars. We were told that if you are driving a car and hit another car, you should not stop. Instead, go directly to a police station and return with the police. Generally, people drive close to home, and if people on the street see that your car either hit or was hit by their relative's car, they might lynch you as the foreigner. The driver of the larger vehicle generally pays for damages to the smaller vehicle, so if a truck is rear-ended by a car (and the law says the rear vehicle is liable in such cases), the truck driver pays for the damages to the car. Again, this is the practice, not the law. And, Thais generally don't involve the courts.

In the City of Phitsanuluk, I experienced my very first rickshaw ride. Rickshaws are carts pulled by a bicyclist that function as a taxi. The cyclist was an old man and asked me if he could give me a ride anywhere. I rode for three blocks, and immediately felt bad that such an old man was pulling me around. He asked for 120 *baht* and took 100 baht; that was only four dollars. Later that evening, my guide got each of us a rickshaw to go a much further distance to an open air eatery. The suggested price was 10 baht each, and the guide gave them 15 baht each. Wow. Very few foreign tourists wandered around Phitsanuluk, so that first driver was lucky to have found me. The city is a hub of commerce with a population of one million, but it is not considered a large city. I saw many poor people in Thailand but unlike in the US, the poor seemed to remain part of the larger community. It looked as if they were not begrudged scraps of food or shelter under a vendor's table in a storm. Their plight seemed much less desperate and less alienated than that of those who are poor in the U.S.A.

I was in Thailand during elections and our motor vehicles frequently got stalled in election parades. Both men and women seemed to be well represented in politics that year; it was 1996. I was told Bill Clinton had won the election in the U.S.A. and had some conversations about elections in general. People in Bangkok seemed to think it was expensive to run for office in the US, because there must be a lot of vote buying. In Thailand, elections are completed by secret ballot. If it is discovered that you voted for a candidate other than the one for whom you were paid to vote, you would most likely be shot dead. I pondered that secret ballot. I was also told that if you speak ill of a person, you must knock two times on wood and push it away with your hand so the bad remark doesn't reverberate back onto you. Politics have a lot in common wherever you are.

A *wat* is a temple. On a tour of the Wat Doi Suthep, a temple on top of a hill in Chang Mai, I learned about the goddess who used her hair like a hose to flood the bandits trying to impede Buddha's meditation. The cobra-like snakes shielded Buddha from the rains so he could continue to meditate. They curled up on top of each other to provide a high seat and looked out over him to provide an umbrella. The stairways at many temples have scaled serpents (long skinny dragons) for railings with their many tails at the top of the stairs and their many heads are at the bottom of the stairs. The guide, Boo, told us the meaning found in this imagery: "When the serpent's tail is up, you can climb to Paradise." Posted on trees throughout the temple grounds, were platitudes of spiritual awareness such as "One cannot stop fire from emitting smoke." I liked the posters of dogs gambling and drinking and playing cards. Boo explained that the artist used dogs instead of people to show these activities constituted bad conduct.

I liked Boo. She was dressed in blue jeans and a t-shirt and looked like she could have walked off a New York City sidewalk. Boo mixed up her Ls and Rs, which made for a fun challenge: "We went to *tempers* to see *rerics*." Boo took us to a wat built in the 700s AD that had been rediscovered in the last 40 years. At this wat, stood a red painting of lust, anger, and jail (red because these make one hot) and a blue painting of meditation, peace, and tranquility (blue because these make one cool). Painted lotus flowers were on the wat's interior columns, and Boo told us that the lotus had been the symbol for Buddhism prior to the use of Buddha. At a Zen Buddhist temple, people offered incense and decorations to honor their dead ancestors at a long table in front of the room with many Buddha statues. The Buddha giving the "OK" sign with his hand is a pose that represents reaching enlightenment. Boo gave a great tour.

The most common statuary in Thailand was the Buddha. My favorite was at the Wat of the Talking Buddha, so called because the king's soldiers went there to pray before defending against the Burmese. After the Thai won the battle, the soldiers said it was because the Buddha at that wat had spoken inspiring words to them before they went into battle. This Buddha was huge, at least 200 feet tall, seated with its legs crossed. I wasn't even as tall as the Buddha's hand. I liked it the most because the green moss covering the statue gave it a look of green velvet. In my mind, I remember it as the velvet Buddha.

The Buddha said there are four kinds of lotus much like there are four kinds of people. The blooming lotus is like the "blossomed" or aware person. A lotus bud floating on the water is a smart person who needs to learn more. A lotus under water is the person who can't see past the surface. A lotus still in the mud is the person who is very limited. You generally can't buy lotus blossoms because they can be very fragile. So, you buy lotus buds to offer to the Buddha, but you fold down the petals to indicate you are enlightened. You don't smell the scent of the lotus being offered to the Buddha because the scent is for the Buddha. Bass taught me two ways to fold back the petals of the lotus bud, and I was quite pleased with myself. Folding lotus petals takes some focus, but mostly you are folding in a repetitive manner. I found it to be a good meditation.

Noy was a Buddhist monk from age 12 to age 18 to continue his education. I wondered why he hadn't mentioned the lotus petals. He did tell me Thailand offers only six years of free education to children, so becoming a monk provides a poor boy with an opportunity to continue his education. Noy said that if I ate a lot of rice, my eyes would get small like his. I didn't do too well with a lot of the food in Thailand. So many things seemed much too sweet or too sour or too hot. At an outdoor fish market, vendors made croquettes of fish, lemongrass, and chilies and fried them in a wok. The texture was like a meatball, but it was way too hot for me. The bamboo sticks filled with sticky rice had coconut and small brown beans mixed with the rice. It was so sweet I couldn't eat it. At one point, my van driver pulled over to pick some tamarinds (peanut-shaped fruit about two inches long and with the texture of a green pear). My guide Chan and the driver seemed to think they were the best find. I couldn't eat them; they were too bitter. They were so good, the driver finished off mine even with the bite taken out of it. The sum wan fruit was so sweet I had to spit it out. But the pineapple was always perfect. Sometimes you could get fruit juice without sugar and salt added. I did well at a university cafeteria where I had a fork of vermicelli dunked in hot water and served in a broth with fish balls. The hot stuff was at the counter so you could season it to taste. No seasoning was just right for my taste.

I joined a four-day hike to visit the various Hill tribes north of Chang Mai. Cicada (green grasshoppers as long as my hand) made a steady, ear-piercing hum for the duration of our hike. The lead porter, Moo, chopped around bamboo trees and gathered about three dozen bamboo worms, small white slugs. He fried them with salt for our lunch. I thought they tasted like chickpeas. Moo also made us each a bamboo mug. The bamboo branches are angular, so if you cut a branch at an angle and hollow it out, you have a mug. Moo procured sticky rice sweets wrapped in banana leaves for us too. I guess that is why he was the lead porter. Pong was our local guide, and he held my arm on all the scarier descents, so I remember him fondly. He spoke English well and, looking back, I realize I asked a lot of dumb questions. But, he stayed patient and kind the whole time. On our hike, we met Santee, an expert on tigers. Santee told us he makes his hideouts about 60 feet up in the trees and waits for tigers. Tigers can climb trees and love to swim. They can have orange and black stripes or black and white stripes. Tigers are big animals as high as his chest. "Manhunters" are old tigers or wounded tigers who hunt people, because we are the easiest prey among large mammals in and about the jungle. When I asked Santee how he became interested in tigers, he said tigers were the spirit of the jungle and he couldn't see why anyone wouldn't be interested in them.

Animism seemed to be the religion of choice in the Lisu village where we stayed. A Shaman there can be visited by animal spirits, and everyone knows when the evil spirit eats you, you speak with the spirit's voice. The Lisu grow opium and wouldn't quit, so the government shut off the electricity to the village. We were told the Lisu were originally from Southern China. The men wore turquoise sarongs and the women wore black jumpers with pretty scarves. Some had black teeth from chewing beetle nut, but the Lisu were good-looking people. At a trading post, we had lunch with the Lahu, an itinerant people who were mostly younger. (We were told they were mostly young because they were warlike and died young in battles.) I enjoyed riding the river current with the children after lunch even though I emerged with many bruises on my legs. The Lahu people came from China by way of Burma. The women liked wearing necklaces of old coins; American quarters and old English coins with King Edward's likeness were favored. Edward was King when Burma was a colony and somehow became revered as a deity.

Next, we stayed at an Ahka village. We were told the Ahka live close to the spirit world, with the "*ah*" meaning that the spirit that lives in the thing called (fill in the blank). So it would be "ah-TinaMarie" or "ah-chair," and you knew the Ahka had a very spiritual take on life. There were spirit gates at the entrance and exit to the village to stop the jungle spirits from entering. Originally, this group was from Tibet. They keep their wealth in silver ingots buried under their houses. They don't want formal outside education for their children because they want them to remain Ahka. Generally, Ahka look very old by age 40. They use opium a lot and most start at age five when their first toothache arrives. (I found that understandable.) The Ahka women dove upon us in the early morning to sell their wares. Some wore traditional clothing; others wore donations from either missionaries or international charities. The village also had a wooden "Ferris wheel" that was about 20 feet high. Although we didn't witness this practice, at religious festivals, they swing high on the Ferris wheel for long durations to make contact with spirits, while others sit around drinking whiskey and smoking opium.

At the Karen village, fierce fighting, complete with grenades and automatic rifles, had taken place between the Karen and the Burmese just three months earlier. The fighting had ensued within a few miles of the village. It was odd to think of such strife in the midst of poinsettia trees. In the best case-scenario, Karen children go to school from age eight to fifteen. Houses were built on stilts, and often farm animals lived beneath the house. The Karen chief was elected democratically, but the elected person would have been chief by inheritance anyway. The chief took care of anybody in need (such as abandoned children); decided disputes among villagers; and received a salary in Baht equivalent to about $40 each month. The government offices are a four-hour walk from the village, and he needed to go there frequently. Most of the people in the village were Catholics, with animism being an adjunct rather than an alternative. On our hike, we each placed a leaf on a shrine to the Spirit of the River for good luck.

The Thai King Boomiphol's eldest daughter worked with Hill tribes. The Thai seemed very proud of their king. When I was there, I learned that rioting had broken out in the streets of Bangkok, and the militia had fired on the rioters. The king had the prime minister and army general come in and crawl across the floor to him and he scolded them like 3-year-olds until they resigned. This degradation was on television, and the fighting in the streets reportedly stopped immediately. Constitutionally, the king had no power, but I'm not sure what the current king's status is. Until 1881, it was illegal for commoners to touch the royal family. Before that time, a queen and her daughter died in a boat accident on the river. People living along the river tried to help them but were prohibited by law from touching them. It was the 50th anniversary of the king's "reign" when I visited. The Thai give the same name to each king. In addition, Queen Elizabeth II from Great Britain was visiting when I was there. People in the parks frequently approached to tell me she was in Thailand visiting their king. I came away finally with the perception that many saw her as the Western queen, because they were a bit familiar with Queen Elizabeth I; the same name concept was at work. The Dutch merchants picked up on the perception that the Queen was the white people's monarch and used it well. With all the warnings not to talk politics in Thailand, I did nothing to dispel the notion. I just smiled and nodded my head during these conversations. If anyone could make anything of that, more power to her.

Bass liked music by the Cranberries and seemed to consider them very avant-garde. He wanted to know what was in the U.S.A. that differed from Thailand. We passed a car wash without any machinery, so I told him how we had car washes into which you drove the dirty car, and it then it was clean when you drove out. He asked if that type of car wash would take about 30 minutes to complete. I liked talking with Bass; he was moody (very out of step with the polite and kind demeanor that most everyone seemed to be able to turn on at a moment's notice), and we both took away a deeper understanding of the way we could misunderstand the other's culture from our discussions. Conversely, somehow I started discussing interior decorating with Chan and mentioned the preparations to get a room ready for a new baby in my extended family. Chan became indignant that a baby would be given his own bedroom. Chan said in a good family, a child would sleep with the mother until the age of 12. I asked, and he answered, that he slept with his mother until he was 12. I would have been suicidal if I slept with my mother until that age, but I didn't say my thoughts aloud. In any other discussion, Chan was very calm and polite, so I think that was an important topic for him to have departed from his usual decorum.

At the Jeath War Museum in Kanchanaburi, they documented the life of Allied prisoners of war in World War II whose forced labor built the bridge from Burma to Singapore over the mountains and over the River Kwai. I saw some sketches of the types of punishments the captives endured and photos of emaciated men wearing loin clothes in the jungle. Bed mats, about 30 inches in width, were placed side by side in bamboo-thatched huts. The labor camp maintained underground jails, and the captives' diet consisted of white rice with a bit of salt. A fantastic tale of heroism was noted about an Australian captain who stood up for men who had fallen sick while they worked from dawn to past dark creating the bridge from trees in the forest. Museum signage declared the captives endured their worst treatment when the Korean hirelings replaced the Japanese soldiers as the prison guards. While the conditions of the prison camp appeared bleak and horrifying, I came away impressed with the extent to which people can adapt and tolerate and still hope. I was mesmerized, but my guide kept coming in to see why I was still in such a boring museum so ultimately I moved on.

In southern Thailand, I saw lines of bright lights on the evening ocean. These were squid boats fishing with bright lights to attract the creatures. The technique only works on dark nights. On the not-so-dark evenings, there were interesting shadows from the many odd shaped islands in the bay. We were told that the story on Pan Nga Bay was that once upon a time a beautiful princess lived in the town of Krabi and when a big *naga* (dragon) swam by her, the naga fell in love with her, and they were to marry. The big naga set about the Andaman Sea inviting folks to the wedding. A little naga, who also lived in the vicinity of Krabi, was jealous and loudly disavowed the event. When the big naga heard this, he became very angry and dove into the water storming straight back to Krabi. In the process, he severed the town of Phuket from the mainland and separated some islands along the way. The big naga and the little naga fought until the little naga killed the big naga by stabbing it with his claw. A spirit looking down on the situation turned all into stone: the princess, the big naga, the little naga, the wedding guests, and the wedding preparations. So when looking around at the many interestingly shaped islands in the bay, those in the know can tell you what you're looking at. It may have been the rice cooker that was turned to stone or a guest bringing cattle for a wedding gift—all turned to stone. I thought that was a good twist on cloud watching.

I felt a bit stifled while paddling my kayak around Pang Nga Bay. Here I was, across the world from home, and couldn't "get out" to where my surroundings fit my memory of place: a place with less heat and where pizza is always an option. I couldn't walk to that place; I couldn't just get in a car and drive or take a train. I depended so utterly on the irregular local transport to get to an airport. Of course, having been stuck in the phone booth sized ship's toilet room could have prompted this stifled sensation I felt as I paddled about. But now in my fourth week away from my normal environment, this sensation of being far away and unable to easily return made me think desperate thoughts about the world I had left, a world where I have cold cereal with cold milk. The milk here is heated to purify it and is then packaged in cartons. The milk in the cartons doesn't begin to age like regular milk until the carton is opened; therefore, they don't normally keep it on ice. Bass had not tried cereal with cold milk; instead, his usual breakfast was chicken soup. I didn't see any cheese in Thailand. Bass had been appalled to hear that I eat cheese and questioned if I understood where that came from. I was far away from the world where all people eat bread and cheese of some sort.

Everything in Thailand seemed exotic. The serpent roofs and stairways at the wats, the flat-topped trees, the huge bugs and butterflies, the frogs roasted on a stick, the jeweled buildings, the huge Buddha images, the colorful wall paintings, the tall poinsettia trees, the bathing elephants, the water buffalo rolling in the mud, the roosters and dogs that seemed to roam everywhere, the colorful trucks, the spirit houses, the lotus flowers and strands of orchids, the incense and the long boats. Yet on the reality side, the heat could wipe you out, and bugs were everywhere—in your rice, around the bed, at restaurant restrooms, near plates of food set on a table. None of the locals even flinched; the bugs are just an accepted fact; the bugs were flies, ants, or cockroaches mostly. Even I stopped flinching such that after my third week, I would pull the occasional ant out of my rice and continue with my meal. The cities were crowded with people, but people seemed to respect each other's space and take care not to touch in these crowded conditions. Buddhist teachings refer to it as "mindfulness." At any rate, there seemed to be a high level of patience. Maybe it came from folding lotus petals.

When communications became muddled in Japan, locals stepped forward to help me out. It made sense that Tanooki came from that place.

8
Looking for Tanooki

Being from New England, Japan provided a true change of atmosphere except for the occasional snow flurries in April. Crowds of people were taking photos of the cherry blossoms. I saw lots of women wearing kimonos, which surprised me. But, one woman in a kimono told me that during the cherry blossom season, women dress in a kimono and go on a picnic among the fragrant trees. I brought back souvenirs: origami earrings; collapsible chopsticks that I used throughout my stay; memories of custard cream puffs, and a postcard of sushi. I had been treated to sushi in Boston in the early 1970s where I could watch it being prepared and served so I could be amused and maybe taste a tiny corner. It was a diversion, and those sophisticated restaurants always made me feel so adult. Somehow in Japan, where most people devoured their sushi like I eat pepperoni pizza, it was a wholly different experience.

In the early morning one day in Tokyo, I took the subway and then walked to the Tsanjii Fish Market, a bustle of activity with trucks and mini-forklifts moving fish. There were huge sharks and swordfish. I was entranced. Many of the fish were as big as people. They looked as if they should have been able to talk now that they were out of the water. There were containers of huge conch shells with conch inside them. There were buckets of octopus, squid of all sizes, huge eight-inch scallops and 12-inch mussels. The mussels inside these 12-inch shells were as big as an apple. Then there were the eels and two-foot long silver fish with serrated backs. There were flat fish with big eyes, round fish and lots of normally proportioned fish too. At least four football fields of space were crammed with fish, and the fish comes in daily Monday through Friday. I could now understand why Asian oceans feel more dangerous. Those sea creatures must hate humans. I swear my hands smelled like fish from just walking around.

On my way out, on a whim, I ducked into a restaurant just outside the market for a sushi breakfast. Rather than coffee, they served green tea here. It is usually served in five-inch high cups of textured ceramic with no handles. I swear the tea has a fish flavor. I was not crazy about the taste, but Japanese green tea was supposed to be good for me. No surprise, but I didn't care for the green tea ice cream either. Back to the sushi. I watched him cut the fish and put it together with rice and/or paste or wrap it with seaweed. Then he brought the dish to another person working behind the counter who added pickled cabbage (reminiscent of Coleman's mustard) and put a yellow flower in the middle of the plate backed by ferns cut into a geometrical design. I had six squares of a seaweed roll, two salmon, two tuna, two white fish, and one yellow rectangle with simply a strip of seaweed around the middle. It was such a beautiful presentation, and I got to say *keeray des nay* (beautiful). But it was so difficult to eat! The pieces were big enough so that the chopsticks didn't pose a problem. But the pieces were so big that I barely had room to chew after I stuffed one piece into my mouth. Trying to eat it in bites proved disastrous, and I think this is what made me the center of attention for the people working behind the counter. It was very tasty, but I had to leave two pieces and a square. I gave it my all. I hope the cook crew didn't take it as a personal affront. The Japanese couple down the counter from me finished their sushi plates and side orders in a wink of an eye.

Before leaving home, my nephew told me that a local fairy creature in Japan was the *Tanooki* and that I should look for him. That was a good thing because the tourist places didn't mention him. (The tourist industry seemed to prefer the Chinese cat to the local beaver. I don't know why.) This is what my nephew told me: Tanooki is a beaver with big testicles and wearing a large cap with a visor. The story goes that a dragon got a merchant in trouble and was going to kill the merchant because he couldn't pay his debts to the dragon. This beaver came from the forest and served the dragon *sake* (rice liquor) until the dragon became drunk. While the dragon was drunk, our beaver hero altered the dragon's books to wipe out the merchant's debts. Eventually, I saw some wooden statues of Tanooki that I wouldn't have noticed if I had not been looking.

I also went about looking for plum wine. I had a difficult time explaining that I wanted plum wine even though I had it written in *Nihongo* (Japanese). One proprietress added two ceramic cups to my wine purchase to apologize for my shortcomings in Japanese! They have alcohol vending machines in Japan, so if you want to buy a bottle, you can be very discreet about it. They also had vending machines that dispensed fresh tomatoes. The indoor straw mats (*tatami*) on the floors always seemed clean. People seemed to speak more quietly in public in Japan. Their garden sculpture is about the Zen concept à la Japanese. You decide what the rock represents for your own meditation. I saw a crocodile's head in a garden one morning. There were many outside pools filled with big carp. I liked looking at those giant sized "gold fish" casually patrolling their borders, but those circling carp made me uneasy when I was alone at night. I passed by "The American" a restaurant with a 10-foot gorilla wearing U.S.A. stars and stripes shorts that was climbing a pole like King Kong. I kept walking until I found a warm coffee shop with a Jean Miro painting on the wall.

Reading Arthur Golden's *Memories of a Geisha* kept me alert to the fact that I might not always be seeing what I thought I saw. His book notes that Japanese men are turned on by a woman's throat and the back of her neck like one might think Western men might enjoy staring at a woman's legs. (The idea of a man attracted by a woman's throat and the back of her neck led me to think of the Boston Strangler.) On a more positive note, the subway stations had public toilets. Another interesting bit about Japan was the pink restroom slippers. At first they looked like pink bunny feet to me. Everywhere in museums and restaurants and even hotel rooms, slippers were provided for the toilet area. Perhaps because these slippers were stocked in female restrooms, they were pink. After a while, the pink slippers started looking like they ought to be there. But I didn't get accustomed to the view of the urinals in the men's restroom as you walked to the women's restroom. I guessed they provided this layout so mothers could keep an eye on their young sons. But I might have been looking at this phenomenon the wrong way.

I watched a local political campaign in action. Numerous candidates or maybe their supporters were driving about, speaking through bull-horns and waving through car windows. Some stood atop cars and gave speeches to polite crowds. Voting was scheduled for a Sunday. For advertising, election boards were posted. An election board provides information about the election itself and then has a grid with numbers in each square. Each candidate is assigned a number and can place publicity on the square showing their number on the designated election boards. I saw an election grid with three of the squares full. Each of the three squares had a photo of the candidate's face. Voting is not compulsory in Japan as it is in Australia. I think people remarked on this because my outback hat marked me as an Australian to many people who aren't from Australia.

The locals were very good to me. After sipping and semi-communicating at colorful bars, I came away with the notion that many locals thought Americans like me are always going to rock concerts. I don't. (But after returning home, I went to see the Rolling Stones to see what we Americans supposedly do in our spare time.) It was not only the bar patrons who were good to me. On two rainy nights in two different cities, the bartender lent me an umbrella and told me to just leave it at my lodging and he would retrieve it later. The good Samaritan lives on. Even when they brought me silverware, I suppose they were helping me out.

My lunch was served with a spoon! This was the second time this had happened. Was I insulted? I'm not sure. I found an excellent noodle shop for supper. They brought me a spoon and a fork after their convulsions died down. I had not realized it was me who was the source of the commotion. My chop sticks skills aren't great, but I thought their reaction was a bit over the top. I suppose free entertainment doesn't wander into that noodle shop very often. Just as with my sushi meal, all the staff thanked me in unison, and I said my *oish katta des* (delicious). There were small victories such as when I managed to get the omnipresent crepe stand attendant to understand that I wanted a banana sans crepe. This just goes to show that *kudamono* (fruit) proved to be a useful vocabulary word. My favorite food was the Hiroshima-*yaki*, a local version of savory pancake. They are filled with noodles, fried egg, sprouts, bacon and squid. While you sit at the counter, you can watch the pancake being cooked and filled. Instead of a bottle of ketchup, there was a bottle of plum sauce on the counter. You received a spatula to cut it into small bites that you could lift with your chopsticks. They were served at the lunch counters in the second floor of a building with side-to-side independent lunch counters. I'm a big fan of diners so maybe that is why I kept returning there to eat. Maybe it was the similarity to diner counters, but I thought these savory pancakes were great. The sake there even had gold flakes in it like Goldschlager Cinnamon Schnapps, confirmation that I had hit gold.

Speaking of gold, I played Pachinko. Pachinko describes the place rather than the game, I think; big places with video game machines that double as gambling machines. It was all in Japanese and no one seemed to understand my Japanese so I tried to do what everyone else was doing. I got my tokens and sat down to a machine. After all sorts of test maneuvers, I still couldn't quite figure out the functions of the button and the dial. My machine went wild, which caused quite a stir. Everyone—from the security guards to the other players—were talking at me, to me, in Japanese. I feel sure I must have done something wrong. At any rate, the security guards dispersed the crowd and escorted me to the counter, where I was given two bins of silver marbles. Then, they escorted me to another building, where I was given 1,200 yen and a box of chocolates in exchange for the marbles. They were very polite. I can't tell you anymore because this is all I know.

I also went to a public bath. I tried this early on in my trip just in case I was going to change my mind about trying one. At the Green Plaza Ladies' Bath, you first scrub in a cubicle with soaps and a water hose. Then, you sauna, and it is HOT. Then, you use the *onsen* (hot tub) and then the cold pool. There were rooms for grooming, rooms for sleeping, and rooms for lounging. I thought I was asking the pedicurist to look at my blister, but instead was signed up for a 20-minute foot massage. Another custom that seems common in Japan is that people change into a *yukata* (robe) after a bath before supper and don't change back into street clothes when going out, say, on an errand to the convenience store or to the gas station. I just can't imagine doing that. What if I got a flat tire? Similarly, European men of leisure wore banyans (loose, exotic robes from India) to the coffee house or spa in the 1600s. But that scene is as far removed from my world as present day Japan, and they likely rode in carriages that came with a driver who dealt with any vehicle problems. Another thing is the Japanese don't just put on this yukata any old way. When you put on your robe, you fold the left side over the right before fastening the ties. (Wearing the right side over the left is reserved for funeral rites.) The evening before I left Japan, I thought of the many local people who had stepped up to help me in the past 3 weeks. Perhaps Tanooki had set the example. Once more, I emerged from an onsen and was wearing a yukata and sitting on a tatami mat. At that point, I knew I was bound to dream of Tanooki plying a dragon with sake for some nights to come.

My first dog sledding experience proved to be a lesson in team dynamics and self-empowerment.

9
The Howling

The Gunflint Trail is in Grand Marais on the Minnesota side of the Canadian border. My racy red rental car got a run for its money driving there. To its credit, the car plowed through a steady two feet of snow without getting stuck. Its driver was very thankful. Once I found the trail marker for the Gunflint Trail, I even found a plowed space to park the car. The Gunflint Trail had snow, a lot of snow, and lots of tall, skinny trees. I wasn't alone long when the proprietor of a nearby cabin arrived to meet me. Together, we rode on his snowmobile up and down steep hills and around curving narrow pathways until we arrived at the cabin. I was then left alone to explore my shelter as he left to give the snowmobile to his wife who was to provide my supper and breakfast. I looked through writing pads filled with notes from past guests discussing the frigid weather and their outdoor sports. I had chocolate cake for dessert that evening before retiring to the sauna. I had just arrived and already felt like I had reached my adventure limit. By the way, the coffee is good in Minnesota provided you take it black.

The next morning we snowmobiled a ways to a clearing where we waited until a truck pulling a huge trailer of stacked dog houses joined us. The musher, Arleigh, and another guest jumped down from the truck. I don't think he ever actually introduced himself as "the musher," but I considered him the professional, and it seemed that musher was an appropriate title. Arleigh owned the kennel where the dogs lived, and although I felt anxious looking at the locked dog boxes, I was relieved that he seemed to treat the dogs very well. Arleigh said he was taking the trip with only two guests because he wanted to give his dogs the opportunity to run. We watched him pull three big sleds off the roof of his truck and then begin to take the dogs out one by one, fastening on their harness so they could be hitched to a sled. Then, we all joined in to help get the dogs out and then harnessed and then hitched to a rope connected to a sled. Some dogs were timid getting out and some jumped out as soon as the door opened. When the dogs were all in position, we loaded our gear and the dogs' supplies into our sleds.

Each sled had a canvas cover over a roomy compartment designed to hold gear. I stood in back of the sled on the rear skids holding onto a horizontal rail that spanned two vertical poles. It reminded me of holding onto a lawn mower. Between the skids on which I was standing was another horizontal rod that acted as a brake when I stepped on it. If we stopped the sled to get off the skids, we had an emergency brake that was a heavy hook to be thrown into the snow. In front of my sled were three pairs of excited dogs. They were in a partying mood. Their bark, though, was like a wolf's howl, and I think they were competing for the Loudest Howler distinction. They howled in some sort of order, which I couldn't quite figure out. I was given instructions: step on the brake when you are taking a corner; otherwise, my sled would tip over. That seemed easy enough. Leaving my snowmobile driver as she was waving goodbye, I cleared my throat and the dogs jumped out and away. The entire time I was riding the sled, each dog's ears were up and leaning back toward me listening for what I might say. I tried not to say too much because just a "good work" could put them into high gear.

On that first day, sledding down the steep and narrow pathways was almost my undoing. The dogs would hug the inside (to shorten the distance I suppose), and the sled would turned on its side. When that happened, I was consistently tossed some distance into the snow. Luckily, I was perfecting my crash technique. We were having an early winter thaw so the snow was sleek, and travel time was about 14 miles an hour so the crashing was fast and furious. I even flew off the sled going over wide, hilly expanses. I confess, though, that riding fast over the hilly terrain was so much fun that I probably didn't brake as much as I could have. The wind would just pick me up under my arms and toss me to the ground. One time as I was getting back on the sled after a flying fall, the dogs started running before I was ready. I let out a blood-curdling scream worthy of the best film noir horror scenes. I didn't know I had it in me.

The musher was very good and considerate on the trail. Descending steep narrow paths, he would pull over and wait for me so that my team would go down on the outside of the hill, which permitted me to stay upright. This started on the second day and was much appreciated. I think I gave him pause when I said I wanted to call a taxi to get back to civilization on the morning of Day Two. Either I wasn't doing it right, or I must be very light for a dog sled team. Even with boots, I don't go much over a 125 pounds and that is with flab. The six dogs just loved to run. I remember spending a great deal of time squatting down on the brake bar with all my weight, concentrating with my full being on my mantra, HEAVY, but the dogs kept on running. The other guest and the musher had sleds pulled by 12 and 18 dogs. I was so glad my sled had a team of just six dogs.

It was an awesome team of six dogs. The lead dog was Wyoming; a scrappy reddish brown male who looked like he definitely would have worn a black, leather jacket if he had been human. He ran next to

Westy, a slender female whose white coat had stylish splotches of reddish brown. The next to follow were Mudflap (a reddish brown male) and Lenore (a white female). Then, the two closest to my sled, the dogs I had to take care not to ram with the sled were Buddy (male) and Coyote (female). They seemed a bit bulkier than the front rows, but it may have been their black and white fur. Buddy was the friendliest and was always amenable to play. Between the dogs and me was the sled covered with green canvas; it was about six feet in length. I felt like the team mascot, and the dogs did seem to take me in as one of their own. When I would lose hold of the sled and crash to the ground, they not only stopped but came back to look at me and always seemed concerned. Of course, I howled with them. That may have helped cement our connection.

When we stopped for lunch, the musher took the sack out of my sled and tore it open with his knife. Then, he tossed out chunks of what looked like frozen ground meat to the team. They liked that. After everyone got a chunk, he gave the crumbs to Wyoming. I thought that was fair. Sometimes two dogs would get annoyed with each other and turn on each other viciously. I was told to break up fights with my booted foot. The musher explained that the dogs would not bite people as fiercely as they would each other. I was wearing huge pack boots, so that was fine with me. Looking at the snowy expanse, I felt as though I had as much space to wander about as I could ever want; at least until I stepped off the trail. The snow was incredibly deep, and I didn't have snowshoes. I could not believe how deep it really was. Snowmobiles groomed the trails, and I had mistakenly assumed a heavy layer of ice crusted over all the snow that I could see. I decided not to wander off. Besides, I was on a team for this journey.

I was glad I didn't leave the trail after the first night. It was beautiful in that world of white. We stopped at a

The Line Up

```
┌────────┐         ┌──────────┐
│ Westy  │─────────│ Wyoming  │
└────┬───┘         └────┬─────┘
     │                  │
┌────┴────┐        ┌────┴─────┐
│ Lenore  │────────│ Mudflap  │
└────┬────┘        └────┬─────┘
     │                  │
┌────┴────┐        ┌────┴─────┐
│ Coyote  │        │  Buddy   │
└─────┬───┘        └──────────┘
      │
    ┌─┴──┐
    │ Me │
    └────┘
```

yurt on the second night. A yurt is a Mongolian-style enclosure and looked to me like a big Hostess cupcake. Before supper, I unhitched the dogs from the sled, removed their harnesses and hooked their collars along a chain with the rest of the sled dogs. Then I went down a hill to get water from the frozen lake for the dogs' supper, which was a warm green gruel that the musher prepared. (This was an arduous chore as the empty bucket was already feeling heavy. But on my way to that ice-covered water, I saw a pine marten and heard a pileated woodpecker!) After the dogs were fed, I sprinkled hay around them and went inside the yurt, where we had a delicious supper from a Mongolian Hot Pot. In the morning, the musher prepared a cold, wet meal for the dogs. They got so excited when the food was being prepared. My job was to set the bowls down in front of the dogs. Eventually, there were 10 bowls in front of 10 dogs. When the bowls were licked clean, I collected them to set filled bowls in front of the next set of dogs that were waiting to be fed. As I set each bowl down, I was very concerned that a dog might get missed or lose out to a double-dipper. (I had heard that waitressing could be stressful.) After finishing my breakfast, I put the harnesses on the dogs, put them on leads in front of my sled and another day began. For that day and the next, being a mascot felt a bit less stressful, but I was ever alert.

I learned as I was leaving that those dogs had never pulled a sled together, so maybe I was just another new team member like the rest. I remember feeling guilty—like a deserter—when it was time to leave my team. They were to return to their kennels, and I was to return to Duluth. I can only hope the team sensed my thankfulness for their kindness and professionalism. They seemed in much better shape from the experience than I was. Maybe that was because they were running, while I was tensing. When I reached my hotel, I photographed my black and blue knees in the mirror. My limbs were aching and yet somehow I felt numb from the experience. Managing a dogsled, like so many other things in life, was not as easy as it looked. But I had learned how to howl. And the howling was reaffirming that I was alive, that I had a voice, and that I was connected to other living things and part of something greater than just me. They say dogs see in black and white, but hear better than people. I feel certain the team would appreciate my reminiscences of the Howling.

Vietnam reminded me that life is not always as it seems.

10
Not Same

I often ask travelers about their favorite destinations, and Vietnam kept making their lists. So I thought I would give it a try. Vietnam was previously a French colony, and baskets of fresh bread loaves were brought to market every day, which made Southeast Asia a much more comfortable place than I had ever known it to be before. Scenery-wise, it was a place of many shades of green. People were friendly, and I was never far from the beach. Vietnam is a coastal country shaped like a long, stretched-out letter S. It has existed as a unified culture for thousands of years despite its odd land configuration, with different cultures living inland from that S shape. I visited Vietnam in the Year of the Horse.

There were amazing sights all over the urban areas of Vietnam. In Saigon, I walked down a street lined with mango trees. The market had baskets of pig tails and baskets of fish tails and bowls of tripe. White pigs with flapping ears in pens and on trucks were abundant. A motorcycle parked outside the market had a basket stuffed with about 20 white ducks. Motorcycles transported pairs of pink pigs, each a yard long and tied separately onto either side of the back wheel. Women rode bicycles or motorbikes while wearing long gloves and scarves tied about their faces. They wore such garb to keep the sun from tanning them; in Vietnam, pale skin is considered beautiful. The long gloves looked glamorous, but the scarves over their faces reminded me of bandits. The men gave the women strong competition as sights to behold. A man on a motorbike was carrying a stack of 50 huge picture frames stacked horizontally with one placed vertically in the middle of the stack. Another two men rode on a motorbike with a 3x6 foot glass mirror in between them in fast, heavy, and free-for-all traffic. It is just a great place to people watch.

The driving style in Vietnam involves a lot of horn tooting, which can be frantic. When crossing the street, once you commit yourself, it is important to follow through. Vietnam's population is about 80 million. An average of 800 traffic accidents occur each month. Accident death rates are rising as more motor vehicles replace bicycles. The law requires those riding motorbikes outside of big cities to wear helmets, but there are very few helmets on the road. A guide told me that people say the helmets block their vision and obstruct their hearing, so they would rather pay the fine than wear a helmet. In my advance preparation for this trip, I read you need four things to drive in Vietnam: (1) a good horn, (2) good brakes, (3) good insurance and (4) good luck.

"Same, same" and "not same" became the mainstay of my tourist lexicon in Vietnam; people assured me with "same, same" and warned me with "not same." I don't recall exactly what situations fit in which category. But here are some examples: A photo exhibit of Ho Chi Minh City featured black and white photos of people in and around the city, and I could have been at home walking around that clean and polished inside exhibit. Same, same. Outside the nearby post office, a vendor in a conical hat gave me a cookie; it was a vanilla-flavored waffle cookie with the texture of *pizzelles*. That never happens at home. Not same. Saigon is three times bigger than Hanoi, and Hanoi is three times older than Saigon. They say the population in Saigon is seven million, but the official count is five million. Same, same.

Regulations in the hotel in Hoi An included: "No stinking things or even prostitutes in room." At the squat toilets, you need to add a scoop of water to "flush" the bowl. In homes, you don't sit on blankets, because people put them over their faces when they sleep. And you sleep with your head, not your feet, pointed toward the family altar. A two-child per family law is in effect in Vietnam. Coffee is served with a drip cup and slowly brews until you have an inch of very strong black coffee. I used a teaspoon of sugar to tone it down. They have expensive coffee here, which they referred to as weasel coffee. They feed the coffee beans to a weasel, but the weasel does not digest it. They subsequently collect the beans from the weasel's excrement and roast them. The Saigon River used to have crocodiles, but they have all been fished out. Although the river no longer has crocodiles, the riverboats have red eyes painted on the front. The idea was that the crocodile would see the eyes and think—"That croc is bigger than I am." The Floating Market in the Mekong Delta featured vertical poles on which the boats displayed samples of what was for sale on that boat. A pole with carrots tied to it and with a pineapple tied further down would be a boat selling carrots and pineapples. People row boats forward, while standing with the oars crossed over each other, much like "Double Dutch" jump rope. On some rivers, people row with their feet (wearing socks) to give their arms a rest. Not same.

My boat tour of the Mekong Delta included a homestay. Where I stayed, the homeowner had pythons: one large snake and two cages with younger snakes. He sold the snakes for their skin. He also had three young crocodiles in his yard, but said he would move those to covered enclosures when they became larger. He had a cage filled with fruit bats and said that the students who spend overnights at his home enjoyed his bat stew. One bat costs about 15 dollars. He was 45 years old and made his living raising fruit. He also had a pet monkey, a cow, rabbits, pheasants, and many other birds. As I was admiring a blackish bird with a red head, it came after me. The bird put its large, red foot with three talons on my foot and pecked at my toes with its beak. Ouch! I came away with two punctures. (At home, they seemed to be stifling a sneer at my account of being attacked by the chicken.)

Historical sites specific to the Vietnam War included the Cu Chi Tunnels, which were very claustrophobic. The Viet Cong used these tunnels to carry out hit-and-run attacks against the Americans during the war. They would put termite mounds at tunnel entrances for camouflage. Our guides showed us harsh-looking booby traps that involved the victim falling onto bamboo spears, sharp bamboo sticks tipped in cow dung to make them poisonous. Doors to the tunnels were rigged so that if you didn't lift them correctly, you set off a grenade. While not encountering any grenades, one tunnel entrance had a trip rope for us tourists that set off a loud bang. We jumped! A guide lifted a manhole cover camouflaged with leaves as it sat on the forest floor and showed us another tunnel entrance. He demonstrated going down feet first into a 24x10 inch hole in the ground which led to a tunnel. Then it was our turn to go in through this entrance. Some people in the group couldn't fit in the hole. It was quite a drop in and then you had to lift yourself back up, which I found very challenging. The tunnels also had poor ventilation as air was taken in via bamboo sticks that were stuck up through the ground. The two manikins of Viet Cong soldiers showed them as very short to my 5 foot 5 inch height. The manhole entrance must have been an even more challenging exit for them. The soldier's uniform consisted of merely a scarf worn around the neck. The guide said female soldiers had been volunteers. At the end of the tour, we were ushered into a replica of a tunnel kitchen and given hot tea and tapioca.

The U.S.A. Embassy is on the same site where its predecessor sat, where the infamous helicopter evacuation of U.S. personnel occurred when Saigon fell to the

Viet Cong. The code for the evacuation included radio airplay of Bing Crosby's "I'm Dreaming of a White Christmas." One guide talked about his experience when he was six years old during the time of the Tet Offensive in 1968. The Americans had warned the people of his village that it would be bombed the next day so they had to leave. Going to the refugee camp, his father took his grandparents while his mother took the children. (His father was a teacher and was not in the army because he had only one leg.) His mother carried two-year-old twins, and the guide walked with his four-year-old brother. He was very tired but not scared because he didn't understand what was happening. At one point, two U.S. Marines having black skin met them and one of the Marines took the twins for his mother, carrying one twin under each arm. When the villagers returned after the Tet Offensive, they found mass graves. Some bodies had been clubbed, some were shot, and some were beyond recognition; there are two graves in his village for this last group. This same guide recounted how the Viet Cong used to try to hide among the people in his village. One way the Viet Cong would be discovered is that their ankles weren't tanned; they wore boots whereas most other people wore sandals. Another way to expose the Viet Cong was to badger them to determine if they would assume a military "attention" pose. (Maybe that was a conditioned reaction engrained by army drill sergeants.) When the Viet Cong captured this guide's village, they ordered the villagers to come out of their houses telling them that after several days in re-education camp, they would be released. The villagers who followed those orders were never seen again. He also said Korean soldiers killed Vietnamese indiscriminately, but such atrocities were never recorded because the Korean Army would not allow press or photos. It didn't sound like a good time.

The War Remnants Museum was intense. Tanks, helicopters, and machine guns sat in the courtyard. More than seven million bombs were dropped on Vietnam and 75,000 liters of defoliants were sprayed over the country. The U.S.A. government estimates that it spent 353 billion dollars on the Vietnam War and that three million Vietnamese were killed and four million were injured. More than 58,000 American Army personnel died. The museum had dozens of quotes from statesmen after the war. For example, Robert S. McNamara, the US Secretary of Defense under Presidents Kennedy and Johnson wrote of the war: "Yet we were wrong, terribly wrong. We owe it to future generations to explain why." One exhibit displayed data about efforts to overthrow the Republic of Vietnam after the Americans evacuated and the Viet Cong had formed a unified government. Another exhibit room was plastered with pictures made by school children illustrating their thoughts on war and peace. The most interesting exhibit focused on international opposition to the American War, as they call it there. It included a piece from Castro in Cuba, pictures of the Kent State student demonstrations, and stories of U.S. soldiers who refused to continue fighting the Vietnamese people and destroying their communities while they were still serving in the country. Although the international opposition was a very moving exhibit, the most wrenching was a gallery of brutal photos showing the deforestation and human deformation caused by the U.S.A. spreading of Agent Orange. It was sad to think such horrors could have been averted but weren't. Another exhibit paid tribute to photojournalists killed in the war. Each photographer was pictured with a biography and a sampling of his or her work. Their photos made war more of a human-interest story rather than a tally of the number of villages controlled by each side. These were amazing photos of war, nothing like what you see in the press today.

Another haunting exhibit showed photos of American soldiers and South Vietnamese soldiers committing atrocities against Vietnamese people—soldiers shooting children, torturing people in rice fields, and extorting confessions. The museum marker said this exhibit was not meant to incite hatred but rather to encourage learning from history. One photo showed six American soldiers posing with some decapitated heads for a "souvenir" photo. The museum sign said these images were not meant to bash Americans but to show what war can do to people. The museum contended: "If we truly remember, we won't tolerate another such disaster on the planet." (Reading that, it dawned on me how accustomed I had become to the glorification of war). The final exhibit I viewed was a replica of a Viet Cong prison during the war. It had 10x12 feet cells for up to 14 people with no toilet facilities, no sink, and no windows unless you count the 8x3 inch slit toward the top of the door. Guards walked above on catwalks. Between prison cells, instruments of torture were displayed. Looking into a cell from a slit in a closed door made the horror of it very real. I had to leave the museum so I could breath. Some say the War Remnants Museum is located in Saigon (Ho Chi Minh City) to remind the South of which side won the war.

Lunch had its own type of war remnant in that restaurants often would have a framed black and white photo of Ho Chi Minh (wearing an army shirt) prominently displayed on the wall. Chairman Ho's mausoleum is in Hanoi. The body was set out for a wake in a center room, and it was very much like a wax museum. We were told the body of Chairman Ho goes to Russia for two months each year to receive new make-up. The mausoleum guide said they didn't cremate Ho Chi Minh because the South Vietnamese didn't get to see him alive, as he had died before reunification. The guide said they go to see his body now, and many cry when they encounter him. Hmmm. When Ho Chi Minh came to power, he built a stilt house for his residence—much like many other houses in Vietnam—after declaring the governor's residence too opulent. The governor's mansion is indeed ostentatious, and a sign said the government currently houses visiting foreign dignitaries there. Ho Chi Minh's photo is on the monetary notes called *duang*. The country's flag is a red square with a yellow star in the middle.

Another interesting site in Vietnam was the *My Son* ruins, a World Heritage UNESCO site. In the 1800s, French archeologists discovered the ruins of My Son beneath the over brush. These were ruins of temple-tower structures mostly built by the Chams from 600 to 1200 A.D. While the Chams worshipped a male god, the people in Southern Vietnam worshipped a female god. This caused some hostility between the two groups. In perhaps an effort to lessen that hostility, the Cham King dedicated this valley surrounded by mountains as a place set aside for worship by all. The Cham King was Hindu, and his statuary and reliefs show Shiva the God of War and Ranesh the God of Happiness. The Cham believed the Hindu god Shiva was the first Cham King, so worshipping Shiva as a deceased king paralleled the ancestor worship still prevalent in Vietnam today. Significant U.S.A. bombing occurred at this site. Restoration work at My Son is slow because it is still not known what the Chams used to "cement" bricks together. The original bricks look rusty in color and are in good shape, but the bricks used for restoration have turned black with the moisture. I walked about these ruins during the rainy season, and the mist created an illusion of mystery in the mountain valley that had been set aside for religious worship. Adding to the hushed sensation of the site were a good many headless statues. The guide blamed these headless statues on French souvenir hunters in the 1800s and on kings of yore. The latter were held responsible for some of these beheadings because when a new king came into power who did not like the old king—whose likeness would have been used for the statues erected during his reign—the new king ordered the heads removed. At another stop, a museum guide said the Viet Cong used the statues at My Son for target practice. Those statues didn't have much hope of keeping their heads. I say—the Queen of Hearts left her mark. Another reason for pause at this site was that the guide said many land mines remain in the area. Indeed, a cow had exploded after disturbing a landmine just one month earlier. I stayed on the trail out of respect for landmines and the Queen of Hearts.

At another historic site were the ruins of an amphitheater. In 1833, the king built this sunken arena for animal fights. We were told that a tiger was first defanged and starved for a week. Then, the tiger was put in the arena with three elephants. The elephant was a respected animal, so the king liked to see them win. Prior to this arena being built, the animal fights would have been held at the palace. When fights were at the palace, the tiger would have one foot chained to a column, with the entire fight occurring in the center of a ring of armed soldiers. The arena fell out of use as recently as 1905, but the remains looked as if it had been deserted for centuries. Like the ancient ruins of Rome, it required much use of one's imagination to picture its heyday.

Back in the present, I wondered if my imagination was working overtime when I passed by two live bears, each in its own cage, located next to one another on the sidewalk. I had heard that bear dung is prescribed for male sexual impotence. Along that line, a guide said that snake wine was very good for men; so much so that Vietnamese men didn't have to buy it because women bought it for them. He said gecko wine was likewise good for women. Vietnamese put all sorts of things in wine: geckos, snakes, bear paw... Bottles of wine stuffed with snakes were so bizarre to me that I never became accustomed to seeing them. Not same. My favorite, though, was rice wine flavored with mango juice. We were told rice wine was very good because if you overdo it, you wake up a bit tired but with no headache. At a community cultural presentation, we were invited to try a bamboo pole dance, which entailed jumping in between moving poles without getting our ankles slammed. Sticky rice wine was served after the dance. Its taste was sweet like vermouth; same, same. It was in a large vase set on the floor with about eight long bamboo straws inserted into the vessel. Not same.

Hot lemon juice was my drink of choice in Vietnam. While sipping hot lemon juice, I watched a funeral procession. Monks were in the first cars followed by people on motorbikes carrying banners with Buddhist text. Following them were the relatives and friends of the deceased. Close relatives of the deceased were dressed in white and wore white bandannas around their heads. In central Vietnam, the dead are buried forever. In the South, they are cremated. In the North, they bury the dead for three years and then cremate them because their soul is thought to have departed by then. Whatever happens to the deceased, I find funerary rituals a great balm to the survivors. That has been my experience. The monks in this funeral procession were Buddhist monks.

At a Buddhist monastery, I watched monks chant at the dinner table before their meal. Monasteries have about 30 monks. A daily schedule was posted showing that they start their day at 3:30 a.m. and have set times for specific activities. Kung Fu was scheduled from 6:00-6:30 p.m.; bed time was at 10:00 p.m. One day, I ate lunch at a Buddhist nunnery. The nuns' posted schedule was notably the same, but rather than Kung Fu, the nuns engaged in gardening. The Buddhist symbol that looks like a swastika is the symbol for longevity here. It symbolizes the longevity of the soul via reincarnation rather than the longevity of the body. The design is common in architecture (rod iron gates, ornamental interior painting, and stone carving). On the upper level of a cave pagoda was a shrine to the Mother Goddess, prominent in the traditional Vietnamese religion where one venerates one's ancestors. There was also a shrine to ancestors that had snake decorations hanging from the ceiling boards. On either side of the altar were spears with dragon faces. On the wall facing the altar was a beautiful, velvet-looking, embroidered banner with dragons on either side. In looking at these shrines, so many of my questions remained unanswered.

But I did manage to get the scoop on the hats. The common hat style in Vietnam is conical and great for gardening in the sun. I wanted to buy one and see how they were made. After some organizing, I set off with a car of three other tourists and a guide to visit a woman who made conical hats at her home. In her living room was a bookcase with a shrine to Jesus on the top shelf and below that was a shrine to her father. She said she was a Catholic and that Vietnamese Catholics worship their ancestors too. Returning to the hats. The hat maker gets dried palm leaves and irons them. Then she puts circular rungs of cord around a cone frame and attaches the palm leaves to the top and then to the bottom of the frame. She then puts cut-out shapes over the frame and covers them with another layer of palm leaves. Finally, the hats are lacquered with sap to waterproof them. This woman had one arm that only went as far as where one would expect to see an elbow. She said she makes two hats a day, whereas other hat makers make three to four hats a day. I was pleased with my hat purchase.

Groups of people bending down over watery fields to plant rice was a common scene. Most wear these conical hats. They plant rice in rows 12 inches apart and plant each stalk under water at six inches apart. I watched them place the stalks carefully in the ground. A week after they plant the rice, they need to transplant it. This type of rice is transplanted three times because each shoot needs sunlight to grow. Many rice fields are separated into 30x50 foot squares with banks that permit raised walkways throughout the fields. There was little or no shade to be found. Farmers grow tapioca, coffee, and sweet potato, but they pay a monetary tax on those crops; if they plant rice, they can pay the tax in rice.

I saw much hard manual work being done throughout the country. People worked in the rice paddies with water and mud up to their knees. On a long hike, I sank up to my knees in mud, and it felt awful. People frequently carried heavy bundles on either end of a stick while walking barefoot. Six full baskets on either side of a yoke over a person's neck were common. A man bicycling with huge, heavy baskets piled two on each side of the bike, as well as one on his back was another common site. It was also very hot during my visit. In doing all this hard work in the heat, I was amazed at how well groomed and even clean the people stayed. If I spent all day doing hard labor in the steamy heat, I am sure I would not look so presentable.

Even the seashore seemed a place for hard work. One day, after watching the sunrise over the ocean, I watched many people at work on the beach. A boy was herding cattle along the beach. Two young boys were selling dried starfish. People were taking three, two-bushel sized bags of scallops from a sampan (a round boat that reminds me of a giant cereal bowl). A boy was driving a cart pulled by two oxen. About 12 people took what seemed like forever to pull in a huge net of fish. I thought they were pulling in a boat, so I'm glad I stayed until the end to see that it was a net full of fish. I felt lazy just sitting on the beach since sunrise. But I had been studying the starfish indentations sunk into the sand, and that might be considered useful.

While I passed on the hard work, I gave the cleanliness notion a try. In Hanoi, I had my ears cleaned. Tall chairs were set out on sidewalks and tended by people who would clean your ears for a fee. After the cleaning began, I started having second thoughts about safety, but everyone seemed to get their ears cleaned in Vietnam. First, the attendant went deep into my ear with a long, thin stick. Then, she cleaned a little less deeply with a cotton swab and finally used a soft bristle brush deep inside my ear. Fortunately my eardrums were fine afterward. I think I prefer to keep them less clean.

In Haiphong, a girl selling postcards told me she could tell I was a foreigner after I said, "Not from here" in response to her question "Where are you from?" I asked her how she knew I was a foreigner. She said because of the color of my skin, because my nose was big and because I had blue eyes. I said, "I have brown eyes." After a close inspection, she said, "There's a little brown in them." Then she told me that people in Haiphong have small noses and black eyes. I liked her spunk.

Many aspects of Vietnam reminded me that I was a foreigner. I admit to holding back on ordering the sparrow and beef penis dishes. But these were common fare. I did try the birds' beak soup. At most restaurants, a wet, white face cloth was served in sealed white plastic, and the practice is to burst the plastic by squeezing it, thus creating a loud pop. It was a good way to start a meal. And in the heat, it was good to have something cold with which to wipe your hands and face. Restaurants had a common blue chair set up: junior-sized plastic chairs surrounded low tables. The set-up was bigger than a dollhouse, but a toy bake oven would have fit right in. Standard plastic cylindrical holders with an opening at the top for "napkins" (which looked like toilet paper to me) were the norm. At first, sitting like a giant in those places and being served by regular sized waiters felt unreal. In fact, I would often think—-this has to be a joke. After a while, it felt normal to be supping at the toy-sized tables and chairs and drinking weasel coffee from toy-sized cups and saucers.

Vietnam grew on me. It was very subtle such that I adjusted without much thinking. After all, they provided fresh bread in this part of the world. When I left my hotel at eight o'clock in the morning, I had just finished my breakfast: a 12-inch loaf of bread, a greasy scrambled egg, and a half cup of strong coffee with a dab of sweetened condensed milk at the bottom of a miniature tea cup. It seemed so normal. Same same. And, with the exchange rate, I was filthy rich in Vietnam; I'm sure that had a lot to do with my comfort level. When I returned home, I picked up a quick bag of groceries and spent thirty dollars. Not same….not at all.

A trip to see the sights around Milwaukee led me to ponder just who I am and realize I need a stage name.

11
More Than One Type of Clown

Milwaukee is one hour later than Eastern Standard Time. I didn't quite know what to expect. I had driven around a lot of detours and road construction and blasted a Loverboy CD to wile away the time on those grey roadways. The rental car had a Wisconsin license plate that said "America's Dairyland" so I purchased some Golden Guernsey dairy milk and Radloff's Colby cheese so I would not miss the Dairyland experience. I waited two hours in stop-and-go traffic on my way to the baseball game at Miller Park. The parking lot reached its capacity just four cars ahead of me so I followed the rest of the crowd who parked at the International House of Pancakes about five blocks away, and then I walked across a four-lane highway to return to the car. That was almost as exciting as the game in which the Milwaukee Brewers beat the Minnesota Twins. There was no halftime, but in a brief pause, five people in various sausage costumes staged a running race. I thought of them later while devouring the Usinger sausage of the day with sauerkraut and washing it down with Miller beer. I don't think I had ever tried Miller beer before visiting Milwaukee. I went for a free tour at the Miller Brewery where they showed the beer being bottled and packaged. The heat that day primed everyone for the free samples, and the beer did taste good. The Miller's Time Clock and the Highlife Girl leaning on the moon both seemed familiar, but I couldn't specifically recall seeing them before. I was raised on Narragansett, which came in cases of 16-ounce bottles. But, returning to Milwaukee.

James Cameron survived a 1930s lynch mob in Wisconsin, but the other two men arrested with him weren't so lucky. A huge mob hung those two others from a tree outside the courthouse. And, it all happened in Wisconsin yet. Mr. Cameron founded the Black Holocaust Museum in Milwaukee to tell his story and the story of black people in the U.S.A. This museum also displayed a geography class prop showing the huge size of Africa; the map showed Africa with other continents pasted within its borders. Moving on, I stopped on the road to get out and take a better look at an unmarked mosque with steps that were flanked by life-sized sculpted camels. The Historical Society's exhibit said wrestling was popularized in Milwaukee in the 1880s when it was promoted by German athletic clubs and is still popular today. People seemed very segregated by color around Milwaukee. For two days, I saw mostly white people, and on the third day I got lost. When I pulled over for an ice cream, I was the only white person in the huge crowd. They seemed to know I was lost even before I asked for directions.

The Clown Hall of Fame had a downtown address but upon finding that location, I was told it had recently relocated to the State Fairgrounds. (I'm still not sure if that was true or just part of the clowning.) I found the fairgrounds, and the parking attendant directed me to the correct building. Inside, I even found the entrance to the clown exhibit. At that entrance, though, a sign said that if I wanted to see the clown exhibit, I should ask for…I don't know…some woman named Ellen maybe. I saw a man coming by the entrance, and I asked him if he knew where Ellen might be. He said we could look for her together. We went into the hall but no one was there. He started to wander off as if he was looking around for her, so I started studying the exhibits in my usual museum mode. He joined me to look at the exhibits and started to chat. He was very pleasant. One exhibit said there are three types of clowns: whiteface clowns, august clowns (thick-lined features and big red noses) and character clowns. As I read, he said, "I'm an August." I said, "Look, they named a clown after you." Then, he began telling me about Cousin Otto being inducted into the Hall of Fame. I said, "You must be proud of your cousin." He pointed out Otto's photo and explained to me how that clown came to be known as "Cousin Otto." As we talked, I felt almost mesmerized by his sparkling eyes and easy smile and thought it was so fitting that he had white curly hair. I was glad I had found the clowns. I appreciated the comedy in our encounter even though it was slightly disconcerting to know that I had unwittingly played the buffoon. (If I'm going to be a character clown, I'll need to have a stage name.)

About thirty miles outside of Milwaukee, the hostel in Newburg had pretty gardens, lots of bird feeders, swaying hammocks, and a trail by the river that was full of Queen Anne's lace and dragonflies. The area was in the midst of a drought, but it rained while I was there, so we went out and celebrated by dancing in the rain and got soaked. I was the only hostel guest and had a huge building with 12 twin beds all to myself. I tried each bed seeking a firm mattress. The kitchen was in the main house guarded by the cats. A group of meditative people lived on the grounds. I partook in a long discussion about being who we are and having the time and the inclination to consider who we are. I returned to Milwaukee in my new reflective mood until I came to the Milwaukee Public Museum exhibit that showed a North American Crocodile with a sign saying they only live in Florida. I swear that was the same animal I saw sunning itself on the riverbank; the one that swaggered down the bank of the Edisto River and slunk into the water. It was wide and black with the same body proportions as my Edisto River swimming pal. He must have been visiting South Carolina. But that was an alligator, wasn't it? I had stopped my inward meditation and my mind was being spun around with observation and memory; that felt good.

    The Milwaukee Zoo had dancing peacocks and posing bison. The Alaskan brown bears were playing in a rough and tumble way, but they were well matched so that everyone got up from the tackle. The primate exhibit included gorillas and orangutans. I peered in at them, hoping I never got put in a cage. They say if people can't see them up close and personal, then it would be more difficult to instill awareness about the need to protect their habitats. But still…I wonder how they cope. The penguins were entertaining, but the gorillas and orangutans couldn't see the penguins from their cage locations. Hopefully, the clowns entertain them from time to time. Maybe they get free samples of Miller beer. Maybe they even feel free to be who they are; maybe they are—*loving every minute of it.*

They have some good things going on in that land of sausage trees and elongated earlobes.

12
The Unexpected

Departing the plane, I was chatting with a local businessman. He told me to be very careful in his country and quipped: "Nairobi should be called Nai-robbery." The large men in front of me in the customs line were having an agitated discussion and one was loudly repeating, "I'll stab his ass." I was starting to awaken after that <u>long</u> flight. After checking into my downtown hotel, I started about Nairobi in my usual brisk stride. Men and women would start walking beside me. I would say hi and they would say *pole pole*. I would respond, no thanks, and move on past them. (Did that restaurant have the whole city urging tourists toward it?) Perhaps it was the hot pavement making my step heavier or perhaps some locals were just more persistent, but finally I understood, *pole pole* means—-slow down.

After finally getting accustomed to this city life, I joined an overland East African Safari. I traveled with a group in a truck that stopped each evening to set up camp in these foreign lands. So much about this trip was beyond my expectations. It was truly another world. I had up close and personal encounters with wildlife. I learned "ungulate" means having hoofs, or as a noun, it means hoofed mammal. I met with people whose ability to understand my world matched my inability to understand theirs. I was impressed. I was horrified. I was delighted.

The roads were horrendous. Passengers needed to hold on and pay attention. It wasn't uncommon for the truck to pull off the road all together to avoid the worst holes and ditches. We passengers decided it must be the Kenyan Plan (a diet where you bounce around in a truck to lose weight). As we drove about, we regularly saw small blue tarps set up in fields. They were cloth banners soaked in buffalo urine to keep away the tsetse flies. We saw sausage trees with fruit like bratwurst hanging from string-like stems. They reminded me of trees at home with dangling Easter eggs. It was all very Dr. Seuss. Many people had pierced their ears with wide plugs so that they had elongated earlobes with a big space between the rim of the lobe and the remainder of their ear. Lots of folks wore sandals made from recycled tires. A common sight was the "butcher shop and café" and the "butcher shop and hotel" combinations found in peopled areas. My mind went to *Sweeny Todd*.

Then I had visions of *My Fair Lady* when the Secretary Bird, a huge, black and white bird, danced in circles wearing a headpiece of starched black felt that was worthy of a box seat at the Ascot. And there were other colorful characters. The Topi is an ungulate of medium-large stature with a pretty face. They are mostly taupe except for the yellow-gold painted on from the knees down. They reminded me of dandies with yellow knee socks and Shakespeare's *Twelfth Night*. The markings of Thompson's gazelles and Grant's gazelles were a bit different. Grant's gazelle has a white horizontal stripe over its tail. I was told a way to remember the two: "Grant's wear pants but Thompson's don't." The water buffalo has wavy horns atop its brow like a wig, making it look like a reincarnated English judge. The Donkey is a member of the proletariat ranks. It wasn't uncommon to see a lone donkey pulling a heavy load. A bunch of giraffes posed like a bouquet of flowers. And, they would make beautiful flowers having such big eyes with long lashes and all on such huge heads. I never tired of watching giraffes and marveled over their seated resemblance to my notion of sea serpents. The zebra is the prototypical party animal. Their manes are set in an upcomb; they either use mousse or maybe they press their manes with starch. Some zebra parties turned sour. I saw one zebra kick another in the face with its hind legs. Lions stalked their parties, and I saw a lioness drag a striped party dude into the tall grass. This explained the strong security presence. On the march, the lead male zebra brayed like an army sergeant. "Hup two three; keep up; stay in line." There are high crime areas anywhere.

The hippos lounged in the water with their faces above the surface. Their wide grins looked up at us from their cool pools. I think they were smirking because the tourists come to watch them fart and defecate. Next to the hippos, a big crocodile head was heading for shore, so I ran down to the water's edge for a better look. In a flash, this 20-foot beast was out of the water, and I realized I was too close. I just had time to mouth "Oh my god!" and it was gone. That croc obviously had advance reports on my kind. Probably heard we were deadly. Lucky for me because I know I personally was no match for it.

We stopped at a campground that advertised showers. But an elephant had stepped on the pipes and the water was no longer connected to the showers. Monkeys and baboons walked around me as though they could not care less if they stepped on me. One morning driving in an open jeep about an hour before sunrise, we stopped in the middle of the road and watched with anticipation of God knows what. A dark brown male lion slowly sauntered across the road within a few feet of us and disappeared into the tall grass. It was clear we were on his turf. For a cat, he seemed mildly amused that a jeep had stopped in the middle of his road.

The Datoka people live in extended families. They keep cattle and the children's education pretty much consists of the boys being taught about the cattle. There

A bouquet of giraffes

was no response to my question about the girls' education. All I could see was a world of flies with no screens. I remember thinking that maybe coming from a small New England mill town wasn't so bad. Our Datoka guide continued on with us to serve as our guide and translator and scout to visit the Hazda people.

The Hazda people are hunter/gatherers who lived wherever they happen to be found. That was an address to confound visitors. Finally, we found them. The men showed off their skills with a bow and arrow. (I think they were upset that they let me use their equipment once they saw my lack of skill.) The women sat around off to the side in a circle and seemed to drape their torsos in clothe just for our benefit. There was a dead gannet hanging upside down from a tree, which we were told was the morning kill. One of the Hazda men had raised lumps of white on his skin. I was afraid to ask about it, because I thought it was some awful skin infection. I needn't have worried; the marks were remnants of a hunt during which he had been clawed by a leopard that he eventually killed. He was very proud of the tale and happy to tell someone about it. The Hazda men wore long strands of porcupine quills and tried to sell them to us. When the Datoka guide and translator lifted a Hazda necklace to show it to me, the thread broke and the quills fell to the ground. To calm the mounting tension, I bought the broken strand. (I re-strung the quills on tooth floss once I got home.)

We saw lots of Massai throughout Kenya and Tanzania. The men herded cattle; they carried no drinking water but didn't leave home without their spears and clubs. The Massai men wear red to recognize each other and to show they are not afraid of blood. In earlier days, they wore tattoos with red designs. The three Massai guides on our hike carried big weapons. They said the small clubs were for hitting children on the head, the longer stick was for whacking people and animals, and the spear was for self-defense. Hunting is illegal, but we were told an elephant could be felled with a forceful spear thrust into its heart or its liver.

Other bits of information impressed me as well. The government outlawed female circumcision, and we were told all but two of the Massai tribes have discontinued it. The Massai remove a front bottom tooth so that if you faint, you can be given water through the opening. Fig trees are sacred and bring good luck. Fig trees can only be cut by a decision of the village elders and then only with a ceremony that no disabled person may attend. The Massai build a new house every three years because the wood rots and must be replaced. The Massai told us *Ngorongoro* means "hole like a pot" and *Serengeti* means "endless plain." Starting in 1992, the Massai have not been permitted to camp in the Ngorongoro Crater, but they can bring animals to graze there during the day. This camping prohibition has decreased both the pollution and the poachers in the Crater. Now, if a Park Ranger sees a person in the Crater at night, he knows the person is not there legally. When the Massai were permitted to camp in the Crater, a poacher caught at night would say he was just grazing his cattle. I went to the local bar at the camp in Amboseli National Park where the Maasai graze their cattle. At the bar were locals in traditional garb complemented by a Walkman or baseball cap. They were playing pool and hanging out. I was sitting at a corner table drinking beer. I truly felt as if I was far from home or maybe looking into another world through a hologram. Because they looked very exotic, I was repeatedly surprised to learn the Massai I met had first names from the New Testament; they were Christians.

All during our safari, locals said that it was hotter than most could recall. I wandered around a downtown urban area in Tazania and thought I might die from the heat, so I stopped at a store to get drinking water. A regal woman in a purple dress with a matching turban sat on a stool at the cash register. In the heat, she brought dignity to that store. I thought she was impressive. And that was before she sold me some peanuts at a discount, because I was short on Tanzanian currency. She was about a size 18 but didn't look fat; just substantial. She made a lasting impression on me. Somehow, if this regal personage lived in the U.S.A., I wondered if she might be decked out in junk clothes and have a chip on her shoulder.

    It is important around Kenya and Tanzania to say "Hello" and "How are you?" and engage in some bit of other small talk before you get to business and say something such as, "Do you have bottled water here?" If I barged into a topic, the local person would generally respond in short form and then go into the "How are you?" mode. Extended greetings are important. Maybe this etiquette requires you to consider the individual to whom you are speaking before getting to the gist of why you are initiating the communication. Such an approach makes for a more civilized feel with more people seeming to have dignity and more people willing to treat you with dignity. For me, it was an unexpected find. They have some good things going on in that world of sausage trees, hippo pools, and elongated earlobes. *Pole, pole.*

Zigzagging around Alaska helped me gain a new perspective about where I'm from and made me wonder if my hometown has a bachelors' album.

13
Covering Ground

Alaska is our biggest state. Tourist information was always ready with trivia to help you understand the extent of the landmass. For example, you could fit 29 smaller states in the State of Alaska. If New York had the same ratio of residents per square mile as Alaska, Manhattan would have only about 14 residents. Despite this lack of demographic density, the local police logs were full of colorful tidbits. They looked like they kept very busy with missing dogs and underage cigarette smokers. Popular entertainment among the locals seemed to be to "Get the stranger to ring the bell." If you ring the bell at an establishment, then the drinks are on you. I stopped at the Salty Dog Saloon and chatted with the locals and sipped blackberry brandy. Seeing the crowd was about right, I even rang the bell and treated the house (a whole three beers and one coffee). I rang the bell in our biggest state; low population density has its perks.

I had finished planning my itinerary for Alaska when the Alaskan Ferry schedule arrived in the mail. It was then I learned the ferry arrivals and departures were not as regular as the guidebooks had promised. So I improvised by going back and forth, up and down, and side to side. Traveling around Alaska, I truly covered a lot of ground. After a quick stop in Anchorage to stretch out horizontally after my long plane trip from Boston, I headed toward Homer. About 60 miles before Homer, I saw the very first wild moose I had ever spotted in my life. The trip was already a success. It stayed light until midnight, so I got my money's worth too.

I had Homer on my itinerary for bird watching, but the season had not started yet. (Though I did get to see incredible numbers of puffins at Gull Island.) According to the prior week's newspapers that I read at the local diner, Homer is the Halibut Capital of the World. With no bird-watching tours running, I signed up for a halibut fishing trip. I'm not your classic fisherman although I did catch a hornpout when I was 10 years old. It looked fine swimming in the bathtub, but my mother insisted that I gut and cook it. I had not gone fishing since. I was determined to be a good sport about my upcoming excursion as I had signed on to a boat full of fishing enthusiasts. We met at the boat at 6:30 in the morning. (I learned that the captain wintered on Cape Cod! That is in New England.) We used cod for bait. People don't eat the cod in Homer because it has worms. The live cod flapped about on the boat's floor, and I watched with feigned apathy as the captain cut pieces off that live cod and baited our hooks. He showed it to other boats passing by, and they commended him for having "blood on the boat" as if it was a good omen for our expedition. As the fates would have it, we were a lucky group, but no one caught a shooter. A shooter is a fish big enough that once you get it on board, you need to shoot it rather than club it over the head.

My first catch was awfully heavy and I reeled it in forever. We were fishing at a depth of 245 feet, and halibut are ground fish. The captain told us if we couldn't feel our weights on the ocean floor, we may as well be fishing in a waste basket. So I had lengthened the line considerably as the current kept pulling the weight off the bottom. Finally, the captain hauled the fish into the boat for me. I would say the fish was four and a half feet long and about 18 inches wide; it was a flat fish. The halibut was 12 inches shorter than me but just about my width. I remember thinking it was a fair contest. It weighed in at only 41 pounds but it was an athletic fish. My fishing companions assured me I wouldn't want a fish much larger because a 40-pounder was a "good eating" fish. I also reeled in a 10-pound fish and that was just my speed. But I threw it back because we were allowed to keep only two fish. Next, I caught a 28-pound fish, which I kept. I was re-casting by then so the reeling took much less time. When we returned to shore, our fish were hung from a rack and washed down. My 37 pounds of fish fillets were dry frozen and sent to my parents' home. I still wish that I had been present at that surprise delivery.

Significant numbers of moose meandered around the town of Homer, which made it difficult to leave. But, I tore myself away to head toward Girdwood if for no other reason than the smell of squaw candy had permeated my hotel room. Squaw candy is a very salty, smoked salmon. My fishing companions had insisted I have some and after just one overnight, it had taken over my room. Upon further reflection, I may have been ready to run by the time I left Homer. Again, getting my news from the outdated newspapers at the local diner, I discovered my plane ticket to Fairbanks was useless because the local airline had gone out of business! At the tiny airport in Homer, I waited and waited and finally managed to purchase an alternative ticket. While reeling that such happenstance had saved me from being stranded the next week, I reflected upon the whale skeleton at the Pratt Museum and realized I should be thankful. In that spirit, I headed northeast toward Girdwood.

Girdwood was very clean smelling. I stayed in a log cabin with no electricity located in a deep valley surrounded by mountains. I got there at eight o'clock in the evening, and the cabin was deserted. The directions seemed clear so after looking around, I went out to eat and then returned to settle in for the night. All the time,

Halibut vs. Human

I was hoping I was in the right place. The owner came in at eleven o'clock and then four other lodgers arrived around midnight. The owner was from Massachusetts but had lived in Alaska since 1964. He was very talkative but interesting. He was working on "relinquishing"— way ahead of the *feng shui* fad that later came to the lower forty-eight. He treated me to breakfast, and I couldn't help thinking about my grandmother who would talk on and on and every so often apologize. She'd go on to explain it was because she never had anyone to talk to. It did seem like it could get lonely amid the wide open spaces. But at least the summer nights were short.

I stopped in Palmer to visit a reindeer farm. The reindeer were much stockier than the Rudolph television special made them out to be. Reindeer are more cleancut looking than the long-haired musk oxen. Musk oxen were extinct in Alaska, Siberia, and Europe but not in Greenland. In 1930, a herd was procured from Greenland and sent to Alaska, and now there is a musk oxen farm in Palmer. The sign said the musk oxen are like buffalo and referred to them as being prehistoric. I thought they had big feet. At the museum in Wasilla, the animal theme continued. A raincoat made from seal intestines was hung amid the antique snowshoe and dogsled equipment. At the time, Wasilla was the starting point for the Iditarod (dog sled race) each winter. Posters showed the mob scenes and the excitement. As I was there in the spring, I could only imagine what that town might look like with a crowd.

From there, I headed out to Sheep Mountain Lodge at Mile 113.5 of the Glen Highway. Sheep Mountain was the prettiest place I saw in Alaska with white snowy mountains in one direction and multi-shaded brown mountains in the other. Over a sourdough pancake breakfast, I talked with a woman born and raised in the area. She said the surroundings were technically desert ground but the cold kept it frozen. It didn't look like desert to me. Hiking with moose in the midst of mountains was so surreal. I had not yet heard the stories about people being kicked to death by moose so it seemed very peaceful except for the mosquito population. The mosquitoes were huge and so thick to be startling when they landed with a thud on my book. I was thankful for the warning.

From Sheep Mountain, I headed east toward Canada. I drove a bit down McCarthy Road, the least attractive place I encountered. It was a grey and dusty road that looked like miners had passed through dropping rusty equipment along the way. I decided to turn back toward Sheep Mountain while my vehicle was still in one piece. With all my remaining time, I took a walk on a nature trail in Chitna. The trail sign requested that you respect the land and stay on the trail. But where was the trail? The bear and moose had made the widest trails every which way. I got lost. After seeing significant mounds of fresh bear scat, it was an incredible relief to find the parking lot. My escape back to Sheep Mountain was further stymied when about 20 bighorn sheep headed down a hill onto the street. I stopped my car to let them pass, but I kept my windows rolled up. While not huge animals, they had an intensity about them (unlike the moose) that made me wary. Magpies were everywhere, but I doubted they would have helped me.

I returned to Anchorage where the Art Museum had a display of colorful glass art by Dale Chichuly, which provided a good change of pace. Watching the all-women's ice hockey game was fun too. (For some reason, there isn't much of that in Massachusetts.) Next, I took a train ride with beautiful scenery heading south to Seward. The Seward Chamber of Commerce was housed in an old train car. I had an enjoyable chat with the volunteers there; they seemed so glad I had visited. My favorite part about the town was the polar bear pelt in the lobby of the Van Gilder Hotel. After a boat ride about the Kenai Fjord, I returned to Anchorage in time for my flight to Kotzebue, a town located north of the Arctic Circle.

Kotzebue is an Inupiat town of about 3,500 people where traditionally, thread was made from a caribou tendon or whale baleen. In Kotzebue, I participated in a blanket toss, which entailed waving a blanket up and down to toss a small local girl. It was hard on the arms. We were told the captain of a successful whaling ship would have been tossed first and then the crew would each have had a turn. So I guess I had it easy. They said if you are tossed in the air and don't look down, you should land on your feet. With "should" being the operative word, I stayed on the ground. Also, for the benefit of us tourists, a boy about 4 feet 10 inches tall jumped and with both his feet kicked a ball dangling at a height of 5 feet; we were told this was a traditional sport and current popular sports were basketball and wrestling. The most interesting bit was that polar bears are keen hunters and use a paw to cover their black noses when lying in wait for their prey to better blend with the snowy Arctic. (I love that imagery.) The tundra in Kotzebu had permanent ice under the vegetation and topsoil, but it seemed like a cranberry bog; I think cranberries and blueberries grew there. Sadly, a lot of litter was strewn on the gravel roads and on the icy shores of the Kotzebu Sound. We were 200 miles from Russia but 549 miles from Anchorage. The dry goods store sold fox furs and fox hats. When I saw reindeer chops in the grocery store, I knew I was far from home.

Back in Anchorage, I headed north again, this time to Fairbanks on my updated plane ticket purchased in Homer. After securing my rental car, I even found a house at the address where the hostel was supposed to be. There were no lights. I went in and it was deserted. I pulled down a mattress leaning against the wall onto the floor and slept there. The water faucets and toilet were operative. My first morning in Fairbanks, I watched Sandhill Cranes dancing around each other in the early morning at Creamer's Field. They jumped in the air and as they came down, they flapped their wings. It was a slow, easy dance that fit with the laid-back atmosphere I found so often in Alaska. I confirmed the house I had walked through late the night before and where I had slept was the hostel where I had pre-booked lodging. Fortunately, the signs of "Trespassers will be shot and survivors will be prosecuted" didn't start popping up until later in my wanderings. The hostel owner explained later the next day that the hostel didn't officially open for another day so they were still getting it ready for the season. The second night, the mattresses were on bed frames.

Scattered around Fairbanks was lots of rusted junk on display that was labeled as historical artifact. I paused at each one, remembering similar rusted objects in the yards in which I had played growing up. I walked to the northern most Woolworth's Department store. Because I was so close, I thought I might as well. A nearby art gallery had a bowl made from fish skins that made the walk worthwhile. At the university museum were the well-preserved remains of a caribou felled by an American lion 60,000 years ago. Even the muscle was preserved in the ice; mining equipment had dug it up. I rode on the Riverboat Discovery along the Chitna River, and we stopped at an Athabaskan Fish Camp for demonstrations related to their traditional Athabaskan culture. During the dogsled demonstration, a dog walked around us slowly and barked as if translating for the musher. On the riverbank, three-time Iditarod winner Susan Butcher introduced us to Granite the lead dog for all three Iditarod wins. He had black fluffy fur; I was smitten. The riverboat passed a raven's nest high on a rocky ledge. On the boat, we were at eye level with the raven's nest and could see the four chicks so plainly that

I mostly remember the moist, garish red inside their beaks. That was the morning's excursion. In the afternoon, I joined a mail run in a small plane that delivered mail to villages north of the Arctic Circle. We went to Beaver and Fort Yukon and Chalkyitsik. Not only did I get to stop in remote places, but a good part of the population came out to meet the plane to see what mail we had brought. Fairbanks was a good stop.

Back in Anchorage again, I went to the zoo. The brown bears were very active; they had fat paws with two-inch claws. I took a photo of one in case we didn't meet in the wild. The polar bears were flopped out like beatniks on a summer day. It is strange that the most vicious creature can look the cuddliest. After lunch, I took a plane south to Juneau, the state capital. The city is set on a hillside looking out at Douglas Island and has a street grid of stark slopes, much like San Francisco. My favorite stop in Juneau was the City Museum, which featured the dressing room accouterments of an actress famous around 1900-1919. These included her hand mirror, a hairbrush, some play bills... (Did I mention I sometimes look at the National Enquirer while standing in line at the grocery store?) The museum explained that Juneau had been a fishing ground for Tlingit Indians, who were joined by miners from all over the world in the Gold Rush of 1898; the museum said that schools were segregated by race back then. Another good stop in Juneau was Bullwinkle's Pizza Parlor where pictures on the wall included Bullwinkle, Rocky, Boris, Natasha and the founder's mother, Mother Goose. From Juneau, I took a very noisy ride on an eight-seater plane to Gustavus, where I saw a porcupine walking the beach and another porcupine climbing a tree. Most of the time in Gustavus was spent riding on a boat around blue glaciers. I saw some glaciers calving, meaning a big tip of the ice breaks off and falls into a pile near the water's edge. I confess I was not as impressed as most others seemed to be. I was impressed, however, when a large man asked a waiter on the boat if there wasn't more food coming for lunch and he was quickly given a second full plate.

Still heading south, this time I relaxed on a public ferry, a good way to admire the beautiful scenery with mountains in all directions. At Haines, we visited Fort Seward, the site of Soap Suds Lane. That was where the married officers lived and was so called because of the suds in the lane when their wives did the laundry. (It made me wonder if others were just airing their clothes rather than laundering them.) Haines is home base to many eagles. When I was there, the local talk was that those eagles were a bunch of ruthless scavengers until the salmon start running. It was said they would even pick up a toddler in lean times. (That reminded me of the roc in the Sinbad the Sailor story flying off with Sinbad hanging onto its talon.) The town's only high-rise building was three stories tall. And that's as high as a building ought to go. In Haines, I truly felt like I was in the middle of nowhere. It was reassuring to know I had a ticket for a ferry so I would be leaving soon.

The next stop was Skagway, a gorgeous spot surrounded by mountains. The population is 700 but peaks to 2,000 in the summer. Its population had peaked in 1898, the year of the Gold Rush. Interesting exhibits included biographies of the men who came to seek gold and of the women who came to cash in on the stampeding miners. One newspaper account told of how Jefferson "Soapy" Smith was shot to death; he was a con man from Georgia who led a highly successful band of thieves headquartered in Skagway. I hiked to the cemetery where Soapy Smith and Frank Reid (who shot Soapy and became a town hero) were buried. And now here they were, both villain and hero, in the same bit of ground under similar gravestones. As life would have it, it was the grave of the infamous Soapy Smith that seemed to draw the most tourists.

Still in Skagway, a three-hour scenic train ride on the White Pass/Yukon Route brought us to a summit of 2,888 feet. The train's average climb is 148 feet per mile. The surrounding Coastal Mountain Range averaged 5,000 to 6,000 feet high. It was a relief the narrow train didn't give out with the steady sharp elevation of the track. That possibility seemed real when we passed Dead Horse Hill and were told of the many packhorses that gave out and died there during the 1898 Gold Rush. The Singing Conductor performed railroad songs that lent another dimension as to how difficult building that steep narrow gauge track must have been. The National Park Service Center had a video on the Gold Rush that consisted of real photos taken in 1898. Life looked difficult. But for me, it was sitting in the dark by a single lantern's light and listening to Buckwheat that made the 1898 Gold Rush come alive.

About twenty of us were scattered about a darkened hall. It was mid evening. The flyer on the door said there would be a poetry reading that night featuring the works of Robert Service. Already knowing his poems could tell a good story, I was among those awaiting Buckwheat who was to give this poetry reading. Eventually, a tall, strapping man, who wore high buckskin boots and carried a lit lantern, entered from behind. In a rich voice, he recited. We heard about the lady known as Lou and about the pitiable, cold prospector Sam McGee. At times, he would assign parts to the audience. At one point, I was assigned the part of the howling wolves...*ahooh!* For me, Buckwheat brought the Gold Rush of 1898 back to life.

Leaving Skagway and taking away some lasting memories, I found myself travelling north on the public ferry. The ferry named *Taku* is a 352x75 foot craft with a 16-foot draft; it averages 18 knots or about 20 miles per hour. In addition to the occasional porpoise and humpback whale, we passed some pink flamingos! I was glad to be heading north where the days were longer; Skagway had sunset at the early hour of ten o'clock at night. The ferry served delicious tapioca pudding. I don't know if I would have enjoyed the ferry rides as much if they were full, but they weren't nearly full. I think the 15-story, jam-packed cruise ships might have had something to do with that. At Kake, a 132-foot tall narrow totem pole stood alone in a field of buttercups amidst just the ravens. And I, too, left the totem pole to its solitary existence and headed to Ketchikan. Ketchikan has an annual rain fall of 200 inches, so I was expecting rain. To my delight, I arrived on a gorgeous sunny day.

Ketchikan had many bald eagles flying around and almost as many standing totem poles. Near Halibut Street and Killer Whale Avenue, the Saxman Village had a collection of restored totem poles that had been gathered from deserted villages in the Ketchikan area. It also provided a glimpse into the workshops of some contemporary totem carvers. Whether they were covered with moss and lying on the ground or standing erect with fresh paint, the totem poles made Ketchikan an intriguing place. To complement the town character was the nearby Perseverance Trail, with its old mossy forest of spruce and hemlock trees. Some huge trees had fallen and their roots were pulled out of the ground such that they stood as 12-foot high braided walls covered with moss and provided shelter for the smaller forest dwellers. Beyond the trails and totems, Ketchikan offered some interesting bits of information. I learned that grizzly bears eat dried leaves and twigs in the fall before hibernating so they don't defecate on themselves. Then, in the spring, they eat grass as a laxative; hence the saying, "like a grizzly in the springtime." (I confess I had not heard that saying before.) A petroglyph, dating from about 200 years earlier, reportedly marked the nearby grave of a shaman. Traditionally, people were cremated, but the shamans were buried in caves because their heads were thought to retain power after death. It seemed akin to how the totem poles retained the feel of a vibrant culture after that civilization was subsumed. (Or had it been subsumed?) I liked Ketchikan.

Back in Anchorage, I rented another car and headed north toward Talkeetna, a town by the Susitna River. Talkeetna is where most mountain climbers start their ascent of Mount McKinley, or Denali as the locals call it. The local cemetery has a monument dedicated to those who have died climbing the mountain. While I was there, a trio of Spanish climbers suffered a mishap in which one fell to his death when he slid down a 40° slope of hard-packed snow and ice, and the other two survived but were suffering from exhaustion and frost bite. Talkeetna has one paved road, and my room was in a 1923 inn above the only bar in town. It was a rowdy place and filled with mountain climbers from all over the world. The bartender, who gave me my room key, scoffed that I wouldn't need a building key because I wasn't the kind to be out that late. I would not describe her as friendly. I had tea and pie at the quiet and relaxed Talkeetna Roadhouse. That, perhaps, would have been the better place to stay. Ah well. The Russian climbers at my lodging challenged everyone else around to a game of soccer to get it through our heads that they were the best so I thought it was a good time to check out the General Store. The second floor was a lounge of sorts, where you could look through the Bachelors' Club album with photos and biographical statements on various local bachelors. This was definitely more entertaining than soccer.

I was staying at Talkeetna on a Thursday; it was blues night for the bar as Thursdays were the night of the local radio station's weekly blues program. Many people carried shotguns around town. The sign at the door said customers were required to unload ammunition before entering the bar. My barstool acquaintances explained they needed to carry the weapons in case a moose or bear wandered into their path. The men tossed dice to see who would buy the next round and regaled me with stories of their daring Daniel Boone-type adventures. I was ever so comfortable until I noticed a hard-looking woman, the one drinking flaming drinks on the far side of the bar, was glaring at me. By then, I had stayed long enough to imbibe the local flavor so I went to bed. After awakening to a commotion, I opened the door to investigate and found the Russian climbers parading about in bikini briefs while trying to figure out how to use the coffee pot contraption in the hall. I got dressed and sought refuge at the Roadhouse.

After reflecting over a pot of hot tea, I concluded that I was glad I had not missed Talkeetna, but I was ready to depart. The trouble was that the bar was closed so the building was locked. I couldn't re-enter the bar to return to my room because I didn't have a key to the building. I took another walk along the Susitna River and then returned to the bar to try my luck at finding a way back to my luggage so I could leave town. Through the window, I spied a woman mopping the bar floor; eventually, she let me in! The later departure had its silver lining in that the town's museum had opened. At this small but fun museum, I opened a black cylinder to see Sam McGee and hear the final stanzas of the Robert Service poem… *"the warmest I've been since I left Tennessee"* and I studied photos of the inside and outside of Robert Service's cabin. At the museum's front desk, I purchased a tape of Buckwheat's rendition of Robert Service poetry. As they don't get a whole lot of visitors, the woman at the desk wanted to know all about my time in Talkeetna. When I told her I had enjoyed talking with the locals at the bar, she nodded and said: "Odds are good, but the goods are odd." On that note, I headed down the paved road out of Talkeetna and drove north toward Ester.

Ester started as a town in response to the Gold Rush of 1898. A large-scale gold dredge operation opened there in 1936 but closed in the 1950s. Now the "Ester Gold Camp" is a tourist stop with slide shows, buffets, stage shows, and relics of the dredge operation. At their buffet, I had my first taste of reindeer without all the spices that made it taste like kielbasa, and it was not my cup of tea. A slide show of the Northern Lights or the auroras explained that these were windstorms in the upper atmospheres, and that the Aurora Borealis is at the North Pole and the Aurora Australis is at the South Pole. The stage show was in the Malamute Saloon, a circa 1900 saloon from Dawson City that had been transported to Ester in the 1930s. At the show, the character Prunella Pinfeather (with binoculars and a hunter's vest) described the common species of Alaskan people. Maybe I was reacting to having just thumbed through the Talkeetna Bachelors Club album, but I thought the show was great. The Dog Bite (Yukon Jack and Cinnamon Schnapps) was the perfect chaser for the reindeer and helped me set my taste buds right again. I stayed over in the bunkhouse; the best thing about that was I didn't have to drive home.

From Ester, I drove to Gold Dredge Number 8, about ten miles north of Fairbanks. When you enter Gold Dredge Number 8, you get a gold stamp on your hand, and they point at the stamp and tell you—that is what you are looking for. You walk around hills of dirt with a spade and a low pan and decide where to dig. Then, you shovel the dirt so that your pan is full and walk down the hill with the full pan to the long troughs of water. You shake the pan of dirt and repeatedly dip the pan in the water. Then, you shake it some more until you have only a few tablespoons of dirt remaining. And then you look for gold. I panned a good-sized piece on my first try. Not so much luck on my next half dozen attempts, but it was a good workout. Gold Dredge Number 8 had closed its operations sometime in the 1950s when gold prices dropped to thirty-five dollars per ounce.

With my poke of gold stashed away, I set out for Denali National Park but stopped at the small town of Nenanna on the way. Dried fish hung from a fish wheel next to a condemned river barge and some old railroad cars. I got an ice cream cone and contemplated relativity. Compared to Nenanna, my hometown is a thriving metropolis. By five o'clock in the afternoon, I had set up my tent at a gorgeous campsite at Riley Creek in Denali National Park. Because I forgot to bring stakes for the tent, I put four big rocks inside to hold it down. I found no map showing the location of shower facilities and moose droppings were everywhere so I sat back and looked for moose. With the midnight sun, I finally toasted my marshmallows in the early stages of dusk (11:30 p.m.) because I needed to get some sleep for my early morning rafting trip on Riley Creek. A day later, I took an 11-hour driving tour of the park on a school bus along bumpy dirt roads with lots of narrow curves. The ledge by the side of the road was at times more than 900 feet steep but looked about 200 feet steep because the space at the bottom of the ledge was so spread out. Denali Park is about the size of Massachusetts. We saw all sorts of wildlife (moose, bear, sheep, goats, deer...) and gorgeous green scenery. There were drunken trees everywhere. Those were the trees with roots that couldn't go deep because of the permafrost, so they tip or grow at a slant. At the end of the day, I was glad to return to my still tent to rest my achy neck and shoulders. Driving "home" to Anchorage, I saw a liquor store in the shape of a giant igloo made of white blocks. I checked my trip list: no polar bear, no grizzly bear, but I did see an igloo and the Alaskan Pipeline.

    As always with travel, I came away with some new perspectives. Lots of people in Alaska seem to consider New York and New Jersey as part of New England. The tall spruce trees throughout Alaska just don't measure up to the velvety pines of New England. From the ground, five miles of wilderness looks the same as 500 miles of wilderness. Half of the world's glaciers are in Alaska, but glaciers only cover three percent of the state; I don't know where the other glaciers are located. I was glad I started my trip before the tourist season started. When the tourist cruise ships did start up, I was a nameless tourist, but everything was open no matter the hour if a cruise ship was docked. Before the tourist cruise ships, I had to pay attention to opening hours and closing times. But, on the plus side, I was a magnet for locals who would ask—where are you from? I didn't get to see salmon jumping upstream or bears waiting to catch salmon, but I did get to meet Alaskans and had a lot of space to move around in. I covered a lot of ground. I was glad I did everything I did or I would be wondering if I had missed something special. Next time, I'll have to get to the Aleutian Islands.

Southern India wasn't as hectic as my adventures in the north, but it was still unnerving in its own way.

14
Honor by a Nose

Taxi! I walked out of the international airport terminal in Bombay and the sun fixed on me with a thud and rested like a heavy anvil on my head. I was heading for the taxi park with my ticket showing I had agreed to pay a 100 Rupee fare to go to the domestic terminal where I would catch my flight to the southern state of Kerala. A boy grabbed my ticket from my hand and took off. I followed quickly after him and took it back. He led me to a black jeep, one among a crowd of jeeps and indicated this was my ride, Taxi #789. Apparently from the hoots and howls of the nearby drivers, this was the next in line for a fare. The driver was out cold in the front seat and the jeep's indoor handles had been removed. Once the boy woke him, the driver got out but would not talk to me or in any way respond to me. He grabbed my ticket from my hand; I followed him into the terminal. He went to the counter where I had procured the taxi reservation; he got the ticket stamped and received cash. Then, I followed him back to his jeep. Before taking off, the boy who had led me to the jeep reached toward me and said it was "customary to tip the porter." I think porters carry bags. I gave him some American coins and he gave me a sour face. The jeep's engine was just barely getting pickup, but we departed the terminal and rode onto the highway where the cars were driving highway speeds. As we sputtered along, the sullen driver mentioned that the fare would be 130 rupees. After bouncing in the heat with the complimentary swarm of mosquitoes, I was thinking he could have said 200; I wanted out of Taxi #789. The jeep chugged along on the side of the highway until smoke started streaming from the dashboard, and the engine petered out. The driver stuck his head under the dashboard and started to pull at all sorts of wires. He yanked one wire so hard it disconnected, and he discarded it out the window. Then the jeep wouldn't turn over as he turned the key again and again in the ignition. He kept yanking more wires from under the dashboard to the extent that I was beginning to get concerned. I flagged down a rickshaw (a bicycle taxi). The driver agreed to take me to the domestic terminal for 100 rupees. I grabbed my bag and got in the rickshaw cart. We started off quickly, but the driver of Taxi #789 and another man who had stopped to help him with his jeep chased after us and managed to grab the cart. They were pulling at it and jerking it back and forth so that I thought they might actually tip it over. It was a tug of war, and it was possible that the rickshaw driver might pull away quickly so I was afraid to get out. A taxi driver (driving a regular-sized taxi sedan) came to my aid. He and his partner chased off Taxi #789 and company and frightened the rickshaw driver but were very nice to me. This third vehicle took me to the domestic terminal. I told them the guidebooks said to stay calm in India and just go with the flow. After listening to what led up to my predicament, the partner looked at my fare ticket and said, this says you agreed to pay 130 rupees. I just smiled and said, thank you. They laughed (and charged 100 rupees for the ride and the rescue). You need to understand that this incident happened more than 30 hours after my departure from Boston, complete with late flights due to mechanical problems, which led to missed flights, my groveling for another flight, and finally getting re-routed to Bombay via Moscow in the snow. If I had not been sleep deprived and dazed from the intense sun and frazzled from having to re-file my lost baggage claim that had already taken forever to file, I don't think I ever would have taken Taxi #789.

Through the nuances of slight tangibles, India makes me realize there is so much to life on this planet. Large fields of yellow sunflowers on the roadside made me smile. A local newspaper had a colorful photo of twelve elephants playing soccer at an elephant festival. Ganesh is the Hindu god who has an elephant's head and four arms on an otherwise human body who gets his toenails painted. Followers of the Hindu god Rama wear paint in three horizontal lines on their forehead to symbolize the trident he carries; followers of the Hindu god Vishnu wear paint in a V on their forehead. RomanoV vodka is made for sale in the State of Maharashtra only and seemed like the perfect drink for the followers of Vishnu, but I don't think they drink vodka. They say that India was a Buddhist country for 1,000 years until that was eroded by the corruption of the monks. When Hinduism proliferated, it enfolded Buddha as a saint. The religious column in the local newspaper said to enjoy love and stop worrying about whether your lover is using you because they are. Just get over it and enjoy the moment, it advised.

I visited five states on this trip: Kerala, Tamil Nadu, Maharashtra, Karnataka and Goa; all cool names. Life was much less hectic in the southern states. After supper one evening, I took a walk among the men, cows, goats, monkeys, and pigs. It was colorful disorder that was orderly in its own way. I don't think the cows would have it any other way. The serene or plastered cows set the tone even if it looked like all else was going at a loud and frenzied pace. I was swatting the flies at my sidewalk table, and a cow stopped to watch my efforts. Although standing in front of my table, the cow remained very aloof as though its reality was being played out on some other astral plane. I kept wondering what was up with those cows? Were they reincarnated cynics who had seen it all before? Were they extraterrestrial spies? When a cow stared at me, I worried it might be considering me for testing onboard a UFO. Chaotic traffic didn't faze them. Had they been transcended? Were they merely oblivious? The cows' perspective remained ever a mystery. The cows set the "whatever" or "whichever way the wind blows" tone. At least, that was the tone I got on my tuning fork.

Pigs were the area's automatic garbage disposals on feet. Once I learned the pigs liked my banana peels, I enjoyed doling them out. I could simply walk over to a wild pig—there was almost always one roaming nearby—and put the peel in front the pig and watch it get eaten. But, I needed to take care around the monkeys so that it was obvious that I had an empty peel. A monkey peels the bananas to eat the fruit like people do, and I didn't want to look as if I was relinquishing anything ever that a monkey might want. Otherwise, they might jump on my back to hurry me along.

Food is eaten with the hand rather than with utensils. At a local restaurant where I placed an order and waited for my number to be called, I had the special—Marsala Dosa. It was a 30-inch round, flat pancake with a vegetable mixture cooked into its middle. Although they fold over the *dosa* (pancake), I received a tray with the dosa overhanging the edges and served with two tins of different dips. I then ate from this tray with my right hand. It reminded me of eating Ethiopian food.

Kerala means "land of coconuts," and it is the southern-most state in India. Men would pick up their saris from the ground and fold them around their waist so that the sari comes to their knees; they seemed to keep folding them up and letting them down throughout the day. Kerala is a Christian state, and Vasco deGama was initially buried at a Catholic church there before his remains were removed to Portugal. The Muslim population is much more mainstream here than in the north, where they are rightly or wrongly associated with the hostilities in Kashmir. The many wild murals of the Hindu god Vishnu in his various reincarnations as part animal- and part human-looking creatures gave new meaning to the term Narcotic Bliss. And it made the Hindu religion most visible to this tourist's eyes. Whatever the religion, it seemed patriarchy was alive and well in Kerala. After leaving a show one evening, I emerged into the streets jammed with people, but as far as I could see, I was the only female. That was such an odd sensation. It was like exiting from an evening show at a Broadway theatre and finding you are the only one of your sex among throngs of walking people.

On a boat trip with some homestays in the backwaters villages, I took a guided village walk. When I suggested we stop for tea at one of the teahouses, the guide asserted the teahouse was for men only. When I asked where the teahouses for women were located, he said there were none. The common village scheme was set up so that the houses were on the borders of the island, and the rice fields were in the middle of the island. Sixty-five percent of the rice grown in Kerala is grown in its backwaters. It is fat rice, and the rice on the stem was hard like a sunflower seed. This rice is not planted on terraces; instead, the seeds are scattered on flat land with plenty of water. After the seeds are scattered, the rice does not need to be replanted, and they harvest two crops a year. The farmers attach white plastic bags to posted sticks in the field to blow in the wind. These look like lights in the dark and whistle when the wind blows; as such, the plastic bags keep the rats away! I would have thought the rice fields in the backwaters would be a peaceful place emanating vibes of tranquility. Wrong. Loud music blared from the Hindu temple until 10 p.m. each night. I was told it would blare constantly only for the festival days, but I learned there were many festival days. A local farmer commented that Indian people like extremes: bright colors, loud music, and spicy food.

I went on an evening tour to see a spice plantation. Abraham, the owner, took us on a tour of his garden. He had a warm smile and big white teeth, and he wore a folded-up sari and a tailored, short-sleeve shirt. After the tour, we were treated to a home-cooked meal his wife had prepared. There was a sink near the table for washing our hands. Each place had a 12x24 inch banana leaf set on the table. The rough edge of the leaf was placed to the left. We ate with our right hands and I kept my left hand on my chair. Abraham stood around the table serving the food and goading us to eat more from the heaping platters of food. There were spongy pancakes, crispy tortilla like things, rice, and hot curry potatoes for starch. Vegetables included green beans with ginger, cabbage shredded with carrot, and cassava. For protein there was curry beef and curry fish. The table was also set with a liquid curd to put on the rice to cool the mouth. The drink was lukewarm water spiced with cardamom. For dessert, we were given a spoon of rice over which we poured curd and sprinkled sugar. Then we added a finger sized banana and mashed it with the rest of the mixture using our fingers. It was surprisingly good. The meal ended with papaya slices. Abraham sat with us at our table after the meal and talked of his garden and family. Another guest told how his son was in school studying Katha Kali dance.

Katha Kali dances are traditional dances in Kerala. At one performance, the narrator used a hand percussion instrument. He was dressed in white and stood in a back corner of the stage. The drummer sat on a cloth-covered box in the back corner opposite the narrator, and the dancers took the front and middle of the stage. The narrator described the dance as a way to relate to goodness. He explained the signs and symbols of the dance as the dancers demonstrated. Facial movements, eye movements, and neck and shoulder movements were used to convey traditional Hindu stories that the audience already knows—like enacting Biblical stories for a Christian audience. Sometimes a dancer might wear long silver nails like long finger picks but only on the fingers of one hand. I wondered if that character had been a guitarist in a past life and now couldn't get rid of the long nails if they tried. Typically, the audience arrives early to watch the actors having their heavy makeup applied. The dancers painted with bright green were the good characters; the dancers painted with red were the bad characters. (So, was the Wicked Witch of the West good or bad?) I found myself seeking out Katha Kali dancing throughout Kerala. These fantastic characters in the bare setting with the drumming gave me the sensation that I was at a séance conjuring up the surreal.

Going north to Madurai in the State of Tamil Nadu, I encountered more of the surreal. The temple at Sri Meenakshi smelled of jasmine, and its statues were often smeared with yellow from a paste of turmeric. Some men walking about had yellow scalps as they had shaved their heads and made an offering of their hair. They then put turmeric on their shaved heads. The temple has four tall towers covered with colorful "life-sized" figures that are more pronounced than a relief but were definitely part of the buildings' walls rather than an attached sculpture. Some might think it was overdone but I liked staring at it. In fact, I studied the temple walls in phases because the detail and the colors and the proportions could be overwhelming. Hindu gods in their various reincarnated creations put me in the mind of corporate consultants sermonizing about thinking "outside the box." These artists had definitively learned to think outside the box. It made me curious about the religion, but sadly, the Hindu books I have collected remain unread. On a village walking tour near Ooty, we stopped to talk with a

Hindu priest. At festivals, he walks through flaming fire up to his knees for a length of about 18 feet. He had a photo of this festival fire walk posted on his wall. He had worked for 40 years at the local explosives factory but was now retired. That must have been a life of contradictions (being a priest and making explosives), although again I confess I don't know much about the Hindu religion.

One evening in Madurai, I walked by huge bunches of sugar cane leaning against the walls for at least a half mile leading to a Hindu festival. The festival was being held at a temple enclosure that included a lake at its center and a barge on the far side of the lake that was decorated and brightly lit. It was a carnival atmosphere. A 30-foot tall neon sign switched between Ganesh and another Hindu deity. Decorated elephants were walking about, and if you put 10 rupees in its trunk, the elephant would give your money to its rider and then tap your head with its trunk for good luck. I waited in a long line to walk through the temple only to find that at the far shrine, we were asked to bow before a phallic sculpture being overseen by a statue of a cobra. We were told it signified Shiva's power over male fertility, which was central to this festival.

Outside the temple, crowds of people were gathered around the lake. Around 8:30 p.m., men on the shore started pulling the barge from the far end of the lake. There were many ropes attached to the barge and the men were pulling the ropes along the shore so that the barge would circle the lake. As the barge progressed, more and more joined in pulling on the ropes until there were thousands pulling the barge. Those thousands surged into the crowd of onlookers, a place from which I, too, was watching. The confusion worsened when the police started clubbing people, which I think was to encourage us to move. Then it got worse when all the people dodging the clubs fell back in the same direction and became one big human glob. We were squished in a mob for the next 25 minutes. Sometimes it was all I could do to breathe because of the frantic, moving bodies squeezing me from all directions. If you fell sideways, you would have been crushed by the lack of space. Lots of luck seemed to keep everyone upright. Some people thought it was fun; a group of belligerent teenage boys formed a train and were pushing in all directions. Among that group, a teenage boy from Kashmir kept asking what country I was from. This was after the George W. Disaster, so I just replied, "I'm not from here." I didn't become a victim of a rampage and was lucky to make a phenomenal escape. And, I can't truly complain as there were little children in that suffocating blob of humanity. They must have had it much worse than I did. Afterward in a train station sitting on the urine-scented floor waiting for my train, a hot cup of chai helped to calm me.

In Malappuram, there are temples carved from single huge stones. In one huge (100x50 foot) relief carved into a natural rock wall were intricate scenes of battle, triumph, torment, and redemption. In and amongst everything else going on, there was a cat feigning a transcended state of nirvana to trick mice into coming closer. With five other tourists and a guide, I bicycled around these fantastic works of art. We bicycled in the blazing heat while the goats sat in the shade and looked at us like we were crazy. The goats did look to be coping with the heat better than I was. I just wanted to go swimming, and I was staying at a hotel that had a swimming pool. String bikinis were acceptable but not shorts and a t-shirt. So after being thrown out of the pool area, I went shopping. Not many shops offered female clothing that didn't look like pajamas or loose cotton underwear. Finally, I found a shop that looked like it might be promising. The young boy waiting on me pulled out all sorts of underwear from the back room before understanding what I was looking for. Then the one bathing suit he found was just not my style. It was a one-piece suit with short sleeves, a short skirt, short leggings that went below the skirt and a matching bonnet. Besides, it cost 650 rupees. When I was a block away from the shop, he came running after me. The owner had returned and had other suits. I returned to the shop. The owner had one other female swimsuit. It was a modest one piece without the sleeves, skirt and leggings, and it cost 350 rupees. Like the more expensive suit, it was made of heavy polyester that didn't allow for much stretching and it came with a matching bonnet. I took the suit and the bonnet. If my luggage hadn't been lost, I never would have seen that 650 rupee bathing suit.

The heat followed me into Pondicherry, a small city-state and a former French colony. The pastry was excellent and the empty Catholic Church provided shade from the hot sun. Near the beach is an imposing statue of Gandhi dressed in a loincloth and wearing his pocket watch. An elderly man from Bengal visiting Pondicherry with his son's family said Gandhi always wore his gold watch and chain. He wanted to know my "thoughts on India" and my "thoughts on her people." We were both enjoying ourselves in conversation, but his son's family was aghast at our familiarity, formal as it was, so we both had to move on. Another good conversation occurred on a train where the people in my compartment included a 24-year old man on his way to Bangalore to see a Brian Adams concert. He worked in information technology and offered me a piece of the vegetarian pizza that he had bought at the train station. (This was food I could eat with my right hand and think nothing of it.) We discussed economic policies in India and the 1991 liberalization of businesses. Most of the local people in the compartment seemed to have an opinion on that. I had just finished reading Gurcharan Das' *India Unbound,* so I could appreciate the conversation. Good timing.

On reserved train cars, a passenger list would be posted on the outside of the car. For each passenger assigned to that car, the list showed the passenger's name, sex, date of birth, and country of origin. No secrets there. It is common for people to tip their head from side to side toward either shoulder while talking just like some people in the U.S.A. will nod their head up and down while talking or listening. A woman was walking up and down the aisle of the train selling pomegranates; she cut one fruit and gave a piece to a man who seemed interested. He tasted it, tipped his head from side to side, and gave her money for the pomegranate. He was trying to get another man to taste it and didn't notice she was trying to give him his change. That is when she "ch-ch'ed" at him. That is a hiss with "ch-ch" sound rather than an "sss" sound and is very commonly used to get someone's attention there. Those two had my attention.

Bombay is now called Mumbai and is a very impressive city. It has lots of 19th century regal-looking buildings, and it has the huge Gate of India at the ocean edge. At a train station in Mumbai, I saw a large group of *dhabi wallahs,* each carrying about 20 sacks. A man on the sidewalk was explaining each sack contained a lunch for a particular businessman. The dhabi wallah gets the lunch from the businessman's home, brings it to the businessman's office, and then returns the lunch container and sack to the business man's home. *Forbes* reported they have a 90 to 95 percent accuracy rate. I didn't think we had many jobs like that at home. Then from a nearby bridge, I looked out at *dobi wallahs* working in a laundry operation larger than a football field. They wash and hang out all sorts of laundry amongst makeshift walls. The dobi wallah puts the clothes in a low pool of water and steps on them to submerge them. Then he rolls up the wet clothes and beats that roll on a rock. From the bridge, the hanging sheets looked white. That rock and roll was nothing like the cleaners where I bring my clothes at home.

While walking on a Mumbai beach, I stopped for a snack. Over a portable grill set on the sand, some teenage boys cooked chickpeas and minced vegetables in a skillet. They served the snack in a paper cone made from pages torn from a *Lonely Planet* guide book. The tea vendor was walking around the beach with a thermos and cups so I had some chai too. Still in Mumbai (in the State of Maharashtra), I saw a movie at a posh theater with ticketed seating. *Kal Ho Naa Ho* (If There Only Was a Tomorrow) was playing and it was a colorful romance with lots of music and dance. Before the show, a voice over the loudspeaker instructed the audience to stand for the national anthem; the flag was projected on screen as the anthem played. The flag of India has a *charkha*, a spinning wheel. Ghandi saw the charkha as a symbol of self-sufficiency.

Unlike the main characters in the movie, some people weren't keen on true love. In the urban center of Hubli, I witnessed a Valentine's Day demonstration. Banners of "We just oppose Valentine's Day" were posted on building walls and graffiti of "We just oppose Valentine's Day" was scrawled at bus stops. From what I could gather, women's groups "against love" were burning Valentine's Day cards in support of arranged marriages. In the same town, the bus driver stopped at a railroad crossing where a woman was selling cucumbers. He bought one; she cut it in quarters and put a bit of hot sauce on each. (I was watching that bus driver because I wanted to ask what he thought of true love, but I kept quiet because I had the feeling my questions wouldn't be well received.) Once off this bus, I had a Knock Out beer with my lunch; the label said it was "one punch strong."

(A punch may be more acceptable than a kiss in those towns.)

Bijapur impressed me as a place where a stiff drink might be better than a beer. Bijapur is in the State of Karnataka. There on the dirt roads, I spent some time looking at about ten wild boars muzzling trash on the side of the road. The boars were all black with long snouts and with manes of hair like on a horse. At another spot along the dirt road, men were chasing them, which caused the wild boars to stampede. They squealed in what sounded like terror to me. Then the men caught a big one in a 4x5 foot rectangular net; each end of the net was held by two men. They picked up the boar using the net and carried it off. The other boars had bolted. It was very unsettling—like watching a Disney wildlife show.

At the Gandi Chowk, I stopped to study the stalls of red hot chilies. They were heaped in huge vats about four feet tall and three feet wide, and these vats lined the walls of the vendor's stall. Rather than being irritated, the vendor was proud that someone was admiring his awesome display. It was very impressive. At another market, I saw a bunch of whole chickens that had been recently killed and plucked. These bright yellow chickens were piled on a big tray and their long flopping legs and three-toed feet made for quite a sight. A housewife was selecting one of the chickens for purchase.

Hampi is a great tourist town with fantastic ruins. Shop, shop, shop—bought a lot of jewelry. Gotta spend some money on a vacation, and I enjoyed sitting on foot-high stools, sipping tea, and having jewelry unwrapped for me to "just look." I talked politics with one merchant but another was telling me how Westerners came to India to "find themselves," because they live in a soul-less culture. He went on to describe how some broke down crying in his shop. I tried to explain how he might see a disproportionate number of people seeking enlightenment compared to the general Western population. After much people watching, I stopped inside a beauty parlor for a facial. She started by squeezing a slice of watermelon and putting the juice on my face. It smelled good. Another vendor who had sold me some great beaded belts fetched a white cow for me to photograph. I'm such a tourist.

In Badami, I visited the cave temples, which were red rock caves with large reliefs carved into the cave walls. I went early in the morning to avoid the crowds but there were already warlike grey monkeys roaming about when I arrived. I screamed when a monkey jumped from a tree onto my back; a young man came to my aid and made great fun of chasing that monkey and his like away from me. I joined a guide and his small audience more for protection than information, but the guide had interesting information to impart. One cave had a relief that is half Shiva (male) and half Pavarotti (female) signifying the equality of the sexes, but that was from the 5th century AD. There was another rock relief showing Shiva with one leg raised and lengthened horizontally. We were told this depicted the time when Shiva was on earth as a dwarf and asked the generous demon for all he could cover in three steps. Once the demon agreed, Shiva grew to a giant and covered the earth in his first step, the heavens in his second step and with his third step he sunk the demon's head into the earth. The rock relief showing Shiva with a boar's head depicted his reincarnation when he came to earth to retrieve his kidnapped wife who was being held underground by a demon. With his boar's head, Shiva dug into the ground to the demon's lair to retrieve his wife. Knowing the stories is so helpful. Otherwise, it would have been like walking around a Western art museum and not knowing your saints. You can still admire the art but why the artist added a skull or a wheel would likely be written off as artistic expression, if not overlooked.

A local newspaper had a story out of Chittingarth. It told of a man who had an extramarital affair with a woman. Subsequently, the woman's uncle used a sword to cut off the nose of the man's 60-year old mother. The story recounted that the man's mother wanted to file a police complaint, but local authorities were trying to convince the mother that the uncle's action (cutting off her nose with a sword) was reasonable because her son's dalliance had damaged the reputation of the woman's family. I think the local authorities were smoking the same stuff those artists were inhaling when they painted people so that each person had three heads and four arms. But I bet that 60-year old mother had only one nose.

After checking out a stiff, dead dog lying in the waves somewhere on a beach in Goa, I decided I needed a break and stopped in at a beach restaurant. A Kashmiri merchant, whose relative owned the place, came over to my table and didn't seem too pleased I had shown up. He had a long grey beard and wore flowing white robes reminiscent of menswear from a nativity scene. As he and I were the only ones there, the merchant floated away with stiff politeness to make my breakfast. The tea was fresh cow's milk boiled with green tea. My horror must have been visible because the merchant had a cup with me to show me it was safe to drink. I was also given two slices of bread blackened over an open fire and made into a sandwich around a half-cup of butter. When he noticed I was scraping off some of the butter, he told me that he put on that much butter to show me respect. (You can't bring me anywhere.) When he saw I wasn't eating much, he procured another cook to make me another meal. He said this second man was a cook on a cruise ship who happened to be walking the beach. The second meal was excellent (an omelet with a baguette and coffee). The merchant returned to my table to see that I was pleased with my new meal. By that time, we were a bit comfortable with each other and started to chat. The merchant was opposed to computers because they took people's jobs and knowing better jobs might appear doesn't feed people in the meantime. While not technologically advanced, I was more partial to computers and their possibilities than that. So starting from there, we had an interesting chat in the shade on that hot morning. That same day, the front page of *The Times of India* included a story entitled, "Britney Spears rediscovers religion, Gives up sex." On page 5, it was reported that three terrorist groups in Kashmir had demanded women wear head-to-toe veils and had closed all beauty parlors.

In the Goa heat, I toured a spice plantation. Upon entry, guests were showered with flower petals and given a necklace of flowers. The garden tour included some interesting bits of information. The cashew nut grows first, then the fruit grows around it, and the fruit is distilled into *feni*, a whiskey. A teaspoon of saffron and a teaspoon of nutmeg added to milk is a drink given to brides as a sexual stimulant. Betel nut mixed with tobacco and sugar makes for a hallucinogenic cigarette. It was all news to me. Upon leaving the gardens to go to the lunch area, the attendants poured a scoop of cold water down the back of each guest. Most agreed that felt quite nice; we were told it was tradition.

This trip, I enjoyed my time in India. Going home, I was waiting in the wrong terminal in the Bombay airport. Good thing I got about scouting for information. It is unreal that there isn't a competent source for departure information at an airport of such size, but that's India. Waiting for my connecting flight in Paris, I was struck by how orderly everything seemed. Security guards sat apart in glass booths rather than on folding chairs in the midst of milling people. Many signs informed me of the whereabouts of departing planes rather than an occasional flash about some departures on an unobtrusive television set. Wide and clean interior corridors separated the terminals rather than crowded outdoor sidewalks. I saw *no* bugs whatsoever; not even flies or mosquitoes. (How did they manage that?) It was quiet. Floors were carpeted. The shopkeepers weren't trying to chat me up. Nobody asked me, "Where are you from?" The only bright clothing I saw was the workers' florescent vests for wear on the runways. Outside the terminal window, I saw wide roads in good shape so that the vehicles travelled quickly. I saw no groups of people peering into the terminal, and I saw no auto-rickshaws. A cow walking by would likely be headline news. I guess I'm not in India anymore.

The Loire Valley reminded me of the dragons in my mind.

15
Room with a Turret

I had wanted to take this trip since I was 12 years old. We had to draw maps of France in my 7th grade French class, so I knew just where it was. Thinking about a valley full of castles was just too much for someone who daydreamed about dragons who knew their way around castle dungeons. When they introduced the Euro and the dollar became competitive (for that short window), I was off to the Loire Valley. I had my rental car, the relevant road maps, a pocket castle guide, and an imagination full of smart, fun, colorful, dragons. Dragons have big eyes, long teeth, scaly skin, fat claws, spikes on their tail, and collapsible wings. These were the European sorts; they didn't carry orbs or dance in parades like the Asian dragons.

    I rode around in a bright green car that was so small I could park anywhere. Aren't dragons green? A different ebb and flow existed in this valley of castles. People do lunch from noon to two o'clock. Shops close then. I found this practice so inconvenient and unbelievable at the beginning, but by the end, I was waiting for noon to come around to break and reflect on the morning and regroup for the rest of the afternoon. Dragons like to contemplate. I had a timid beginning with the cheeses covered in gunk. I never became too comfortable with the runny cheeses, but I was enjoying green cheeses before I left. I bet dragons don't eat cheese. I felt almost comfortable with communicating in French now that I've worked at tonal languages and non-Roman alphabets. And, I think dragons are telepathic anyway.

In the wax museum on the castle grounds at Chenonceaux, a sign explained that the king had gifted the castle to his mistress, Diane de Poitiers. After the King died, the king's wife, Catherine Medici, moved in and put the mistress out. Catherine gave huge parties where men dressed as women and women dressed as men and some people came with no clothes at all. It was typical for rulers at the time to throw wild, exorbitant parties to distract malcontents and to woo others for their support. What did the dragons think of those parties? Were they even invited? Did they go anyway? In Loches, at *Logis Royal,* was the tomb of Agnes Sorrell, another king's mistress. Ms. Sorrell started the practice of wearing silk underwear. She also started the practice of women baring their breasts at the French court. Her portrait shows her with one entirely exposed breast. She came to her position (king's mistress) at age 22 and died at age 28 amid rumors she had been poisoned. I'm sure the dragons had nothing to do with it.

In driving onward to visit more castles, I passed fields full of bright red poppies. The fields of poppies made me think I was driving along the border of Oz. I don't think they had dragons there. The guidebooks had not mentioned the poppies but did say there were big windmills to be seen. I encountered none except I did see an exhibit of historic windmills in miniature at the castle of Montsoreau. In between castles, I stopped at the few Jeanne d'Arc historic sites and became irritated that the dragons had not done her much good. It made me wonder why I continue to stick up for them. At a museum dedicated to the 19th century magician Robert Houdin, golden dragon heads thrust through the museum's many front windows on the hour like a cuckoo clock. What did that magician know about the dragons?

Dragons permeated my perceptions; I didn't need to be in a castle to consider them. At the Abbey of

Where there are castles...

Fontevraud, I paused for some time before the coffin of Richard the Lion-hearted and recalled Sherwood Forest, Friar Tuck, Robin Hood and his merry men. Richard's tomb was laid out next to those of his parents. His mother, Eleanor of Aquitaine, went on a crusade with his father Henry II. I think those crusades were a plot by the dragons to get those pesky knights out of their territory. The *Musée d'objet* in Blois displayed all sorts of weird art. In the stairwell was a hollowed out swine full of eggs holding a wheel barrel filled with pennies. On the exhibit floor was a small head of a man with an 18th century coif above a white lacey full dress; the dress spun around and billowed when you stepped within six feet of it. Over the staircase was a wide variety of pocketbooks suspended from the ceiling. What a magical place! I was sure the dragons must have loved wandering about there too.

With a pocket guide full of castles, I was a woman on a mission and moved on until I reached another castle. The castle at Chambord had dual spiral staircases so that I could go down one and not meet anyone going up the other. My guidebook said this was handy for extramarital affairs. It was also handy for bashful dragons. I rented a rowboat to row around the castle at Chambord. I was a bit nervous bringing it back because I took twice as long to complete the route. I swear I rowed constantly. The men who estimated the trip time must row a lot. I guess they even sent someone to find me at one point. Were they concerned the row boat might have been waylaid by a local dragon?

The castle at Langeais was built in the 1400s. It had a drawbridge and around the top was a narrow hall with skinny windows for archers' use in shooting arrows. It felt like a real castle. It was built for protection, but when Anne of Bretagne married Charles VIII, it was no longer needed as a fortress. On the top floor was a long but interesting narration of this wedding with life-size manikins on display to show the people as they were dressed at the ceremony. His age was 20 and hers was 14. Both bride and groom were short. I felt like a dragon in disguise attending the wedding as an unseen guest.

Alas I was seen and heard at some places where I would have preferred to be unnoticed. After I ordered my ticket to tour one castle, the man waiting in line behind me broke in to a vehement rant about people coming to France who couldn't speak French. I tried to speak French, mind you. As I tell people everywhere else in the world, I even speak French with this accent. The woman at the ticket counter looked mortified so I just pretended I didn't understand what he was saying. On another morning, I stopped at a local coffee shop only to be ignored. The waitress/proprietress loudly told customers, who indicated I was ahead of them, that she hated it when English came into her shop. I was desperately hoping they thought I couldn't understand what she was saying. I only stayed because I was too self-conscious to move from my seat at the counter. I couldn't tell you how the coffee tasted, but I'm sure I sipped some of it. It may be dragons have good reason to keep a low profile.

In the castle at Angers was a big dark room with tapestry pieces on the wall. Every now and then, a long tapestry of an important person was displayed that included insects embroidered on the sidelines. Why the insects? Somewhere it said the insects signified the person was important, but that didn't make sense to me. Most of these tapestries showed scenes from the Apocalypse. False gods were portrayed as a many-headed white lion on one and as a many-headed brown dragon on another. The tapestries have survived fire over centuries so I can only think the dragons approved of this portrayal. Or maybe they just understand freedom of the press. After all, this was France. The outside garden was pretty with fleur de lie designs of pansies outlined with shrubs. Maybe that kept the dragons in a peaceful mood.

Dragons stash their wealth in caves. The mushroom museum in Saumur was in a cave created by the extraction of truffa rock for export. Beds of mushrooms popped out of burial sized mounds, rows of button mushrooms grew out of plastic bags. Japanese mushrooms were growing on suspended brown cubes. Other mushrooms were growing on slabs of white muck. Cases displayed a worldwide mushroom collection. The museum was also a producing mushroom factory. They used horse manure to grow the mushrooms and the nearby *L'École Nationale d'Équestrians* has plenty of horse manure to supply. Manure was pushed onto an underground conveyor and loaded onto trucks to be used to produce mushrooms. Tons of horse manure is shipped out each day and tons of hay is shipped in each day for horse food. Eating too much straw can lead to colic, which can be fatal. So, if a horse eats too much straw, they put flax hay in the stall. If that doesn't help, they put shredded pages from the *London Times*. (French newspapers use toxic ink.) The horses are mostly French saddle horses. They are trained to fancy step, jump gates, or fancy jump. After the horse showers or has a workout on a cool day, they put the horse in a special stall with a hot air dryer. I might like one of those contraptions next to my bath. Do the dragons ever drop by to use them?

After touring many castles and wandering about the valley, I started to think dragons might frequent the castle's parlor couches more than the back alleys leading to the castle dungeons. Those dragons have a flair for comfy elegance. But dragons are not stuffy, and I'm sure they are adventurous enough to stomp around any dark and damp place that presents itself. I don't know. The Loire Valley left me with more questions than answers. Do dragons eat mushrooms or do dragons eat horses?

Or do dragons ride horses and show up at nudist parties? Do dragons read the *London Times*? I think it's very likely that dragons picnic in fields of red poppies. I am certain that dragons do wander about art museums. Just because everyone can't see them doesn't mean they are not there. I brought home a miniature green dragon breathing fire.

> In western Utah, I saw evidence of wives being put out to pasture in the desert.

16
Desert Disappearance

The Mormons named Utah after the Utes, the Native Americans who were there upon their arrival in 1847. The Mormon's big push to settle in Salt Lake City began when they were chased out of Missouri. I went to the Mormon Museum in Salt Lake City, where it told of how the Mormons had been run out of Missouri by jealous, self-serving folks. Not a word about any outrage over polygamy. Shhhhhh. While I was in town, the Pioneer Museum included a photo of the seven wives and the daughters of Brigham Young, but it was in the back and out of the way. Brigham Young, founder of the Mormon religion, was wealthy, born in Vermont, and raised in upper-state New York. Mr. Young is said to have had a revelation of sorts, and he claimed to have been visited by an angel called Maroni. A common sight around Salt Lake City is the tall, skinny, gold figure blowing a long horn atop Mormon buildings, which my guidebook explained are images of the angel, Maroni. I had a revelation after a day there. Brigham Young wasn't the only one. It struck me: 600 West Street is completely unrelated to 600 East Street; North Temple Street runs into Second Avenue, but South Temple Street is parallel to Second Avenue. "500 West Street 200 South" is an example of the crazy addresses in Salt Lake City.

At the Sunday morning concert by the Mormon Tabernacle Choir, the acoustics were excellent. I had a great view sitting on the third bench, center balcony, with no one in front of me. As for the Choir, the women stood on the left and the men stood on the right. The women wore white gowns with full sleeves of three quarter length. Their necklaces made them look as if they had sparkles on their dresses. The men wore dark suits. After getting a closer look at the female choir members, I noted each wore a different necklace but the neckline of each gown had the same flower made of the same material as the dress. The gowns fell to just above the floor. The audience applauded before the organist finished and the exodus was in full swing by the time the conductor took his bow. The chorus applauded the conductor and then they dispersed from the stage in a haphazard manner.

   I left the choir and Salt Lake City and found my way to Antelope Island State Park, where I floated in the Great Salt Lake. The Great Salt Lake occupied the spot of a prehistoric lake, the Bonneville Lake. It is salty because water with salt from the mountains runs into the lake. When the water evaporates, the salt stays because the Salt Lake is enclosed with no spillway or outlet. Some huge amount (like two million tons) of salt is added annually by water pouring in with nowhere to pour out. I had read about this in my fourth grade geography class. I had to go in. I paddled around a bit. I was the only one in the water in May. It did taste salty. The water was shallow, not past my knees, and very warm. The air was cold but it was a pretty beach with excellent shower facilities. I had a light picnic looking out at the waves until it was time to move on.

   And I moved on to Fillmore, the first state capital of Utah. It was named after the U.S. President Fillmore who was president when the town was established. I went to the Museum located in the only wing of the state house ever built. There were photos of people and pen and ink portraits dating from 1840 to 1860. One was of a man and his two wives. One of the wives looked much younger than the other. There was a tombstone of a Masa M. Lyman who died in 1877, which listed the names of his 37 children. The informational note said that he had eight "wives" and listed their names and year of birth. The birth dates for these women were: 1835, 1844, 1844, 1845, 1845, 1846, 1846 and 1853. Mark Twain's take on this situation was that he was affronted by the Mormon's polygamy until he saw the women. Then he understood it was truly charity.** (Ever the wise ass, that one.)

The Mormon Church "outlawed" polygamy in September 1890. This was because Mormons were being indicted and jailed for polygamy under the Edmonds-Tucker Act. According to the Mormon Church, this crackdown on polygamy was because "non-Mormons were displeased with Mormon self-sufficiency" and these polygamists were being jailed "for their conscience." Two notions behind their reasoning were (1) larger families enabled Mormons to be self-sufficient and (2) the polygamist was refusing to renounce "wives" taken after the first wife. There was silence as to the decision to marry again when the law says there should be only one spouse (male or female) per person. When I was there, a newspaper headline read: "Polygamy offensive unlikely" and opined that the U.S. Federal Government would not likely start to prosecute polygamists. I was miffed. They were too busy chasing after pot smokers no doubt.

In St. George, in the southwest corner of the state, I went to see Shelton Johnson's backyard. He had sold the desert land (about an acre in size) and now volunteer docents were on hand to explain what we were all looking at. The dinosaurs had made tracks in the mud. We were seeing the underside of those tracks so that instead of an indentation, we saw a mold of whatever pressed into the mud. Herbivores put their weight on their heels while carnivores put their weight on their toes. These casts were set in the mud 220 million years ago "give or take two weeks." It is rare to find such early prints. A print by a Dilophosaurus, one of the first large carnivores, showed three substantial toenails. The signs didn't say what color nail polish she used but the name Dilophosaurus comes from the two parallel crests she sported on the top of her head. With a headdress like that, I'm sure she wore polish. The smaller carnivore print that was most pronounced was made by a Coelophysis, a carnivore a bit larger than a turkey that hunted in packs. In addition to the tracks, there were latticework-looking swatches of what looked like indents from vines, but they were mud cracks. Mud cracks were formed when a larger dinosaur, like the Dilophosaurus, stepped in mud that had already started to harden. That step's pressure sent shock waves all around the track and formed "mud cracks." (I think it was mud cracks that the polygamy editorial had impressed on my equilibrium.)

On this trip, I camped at Lava Point campground at Zion National Park; in other words, I camped in the heat in the middle of nowhere. It was in the 90s during the day but at about 9:00 p.m., it was getting cold. I think I must have been at a very high elevation. I checked under my tent for rattlesnakes before it became too dark. Considering I didn't have to drive an hour, my supper of instant oatmeal and herbal tea tasted just great. I was glad that I had come to this campsite. The drive here had the best scenery of the trip so far. That morning, I had driven 50 miles to a fake diner for breakfast. The orange garnish was good. I was driving a snazzy red jeep. It guzzled gas, and I mostly drove in second gear on these 75-mph roads. Who knew my vehicle would have a CD player rather than a cassette deck? I stopped at the local Walmart and picked out a CD. They had a big Christian music section. And, yes it was hot; it was over 105 degrees. And, yes, I did get sun sick, but we won't think about that.

In the very early morning, while the heat was just waking, I walked for two hours on the Hop Valley Trail. The rock formations on the trail looked like narrow columns of stacked pancakes—breakfast for the gods. I was walking on a narrow, winding path of shifting sand with low bush on either side. Within six feet of me just off the path, I saw a big yellow rattlesnake lift its head 12 inches from the ground to stare at me. I froze. The snake looked for a while and then put its head back down and slowly slunk across the narrow path. I unfroze enough to photograph the last 12 inches. Its rattle was about two inches long. I was nervous after coming upon the snake crossing my path but finally decided to go forward. By the time I mustered up the nerve to move, I didn't know if the snake was in front of me or behind me. According to the picture books in the bookstores, I saw a Western Rattlesnake.

The next morning, I sipped my morning tea after a good sleep under vast starry skies. I was happy that no snakes had found their way into my tent to date. I was looking at the woods with yellow wildflowers and air-space crowded with bugs. (The Federal Aviation Administration hasn't seen traffic like this.) Later, I walked about the town of Kanab. That was where one of my favorite television shows, F-Troop, was filmed. Then, I went on to the town of Hatch. I took a quick dip in the river there. It had a strong current, and it was muddy up to my knees until I got a couple feet in from the shore. But, it was cool and refreshing and nothing a shower couldn't clean. The Town of Beaver in Iron County was Butch Cassidy's birthplace. Beaver was very rustic, and I could see how Butch could have become bored. Although I looked, I didn't see any parades to commemorate Memorial Day in these parts. They seem to do parades more on the Fourth of July in the West.

At Pipe Springs National Monument, the National Park Service offered guided tours. It had been discerned from archeological study and historical record that this plot of land had served for centuries as the local meeting place and the communal water hole in the desert. In the

1800s some Mormon homesteaded the land, meaning he claimed it as private property. A major faux pas, if you ask me. (But don't suggest that to the National Park Service Ranger like I did; I think he had watched one too many cowboy and Indian movies.) Some weeks after this Mormon started fencing off the communal water hole, he was reportedly found full of arrows. The Mormons bought the homestead from the widow for $500 and built a tithing ranch there in the late 1860s. The first manager of the tithing ranch was named Windsor so the place came to be known as Windsor Castle. Mr. Windsor had two wives and 12 children, but one wife and child died before he took the post at the ranch. The indoors of the building were very cool as it was built into the hill from where the water flowed. At one point, the ranch supported more than 1,000 cows. Each Mormon settlement had a telegraph office. I don't remember the purpose of the "tithing ranch." Maybe it had to give packages of beef or potential brides to the church.

In the town of Hurricane, I got a helpful tip at the Pioneer Museum from the woman at the front desk. She had grown up in the desert and said she loved the heat. It was 105 degrees that day and she said it would just get hotter until September. Her tip: wear a long-sleeved white cotton blouse. So, I went directly to a store down the street from that museum and bought myself a long-sleeved white cotton blouse. It did help beat the heat. Returning to the museum, I was told there was a quilt in progress and that the local women stop in for a couple of hours to quilt and chat. The museum signs told of how Hurricane was made lush by a canal that took nine years to build. I couldn't help but sense an obscene hubris in insisting that a desert become farmland and cow pasture. I must admit though that the cow pasture and farmland were very picturesque.

In Panguich, a marker explained that two men had set out for food for their starving families. The snow was so deep that they had to abandon their carriage. They walked the entire way and back by stretching a quilt over the snow, walking on the quilt and then moving the quilt forward to use it like a big snowshoe. I had come to Panguich to see the Paunsagaunt Wildlife Museum. It was amazing with showcases full of mammal taxidermies in motion with detailed surroundings. There were many fish fossils next to a lure collection. There was a small room with African animals. Stuffed birds and skeleton heads crammed the space. There was a display of snakes and arrowheads and who knows what else. Downstairs were 1,300 butterflies. (The owner said he was moving his museum closer to Bryce National Park.) I was glad I stopped in Panguich.

At Bryce Canyon National Park, the paint tones in the rock varied according to the concentrations of oxidized iron and moisture in the rock. I drank in outstanding views of rock palaces and fantastic people (or formations as they are called). Sitting on driftwood, alone with the silence, staring out at it all—is probably why I had come. A National Park exhibit told that John Wesley Powell's 1870s journals included descriptions of exploring Bryce Canyon. He wrote how he climbed until reaching a point where he could advance no further and then realized he couldn't retreat either. He was stranded holding onto a nub. He called to his companion, Bradley, for help but Powell was too far away for Bradley to reach him. Just as Powell's muscles were twitching, Bradley thought to take off his trousers and hang them toward Powell. Powell let go of the nub and pressing his body close to the rock, grabbed the trouser leg and was pulled to safety.*** (Good thing Bradley wore sturdy trousers.) This story did nothing to bolster my courage about climbing around the rocky trails at Bryce Canyon National Park.

As there is only so much solitary silence a person can take at one time, after a few days, I set forth and stationed myself with the crowd on the bleachers at a local rodeo. We cheered for everyone who came out to entertain us. Even four-year-olds were riding cows and sheep. I liked the clowns. The cowboys needed to sign releases to enter the rodeo competition, probably to say they understand it's a dangerous sport and accept liability. One cowboy was knocked unconscious when the bucking bull, from which he had fallen, kicked him. For the first time in my life, I noticed that the animal bucked because a tight belt was fastened around its middle just in front of its back legs. (The man next to me said that was just to encourage the bull to jump like that, something they did perhaps less frequently on their own.) Like the song says—seems I'm still learning things I should have known a long time ago.

Perhaps it is because I spend too much time reading history books. But I like history and found my way to Cove Fort, a Mormon-run historic site. Brigham Young ordered this fort constructed for travelers between Beaver and Fillmore toward the end of the Black Hawk Indian war. The 1867 fort was never attacked. Two stagecoaches came each day, with six horses pulling the coach. The barn had 16 horse stalls and the barn walls were constructed with wooden pegs rather than steel nails. I saw a contraption to lift an ox to shoe it. When oxen were used on roads, they needed to be shoed; otherwise, their hoofs would get cut. The fort had a repair station used for wagon wheels, ox shoes, and horse shoes. I was told that the snake rolled up on the hay in the corner of the shed ate mice, so it was welcome there. I rolled a steel cooper (or a hoop) around with a wooden stick. I started on an incline and once the hoop was rolling, I pushed it by keeping the piece of metal attached to the end my stick toward the bottom of the hoop. I would like to try that again; it was fun.

Touring the farmhouse, I learned the china pattern used by the Hinckleys, the first managers of Fort Cove, was found in the 1990s in Connecticut. Fort Cove purchased the china and now displays it in the Fort's kitchen. In the Hinkleys' day, they stained the furniture wood with ox blood or with buttermilk and egg yolks. Then they used a feather to make it look like wood grain. There was a weasel for winding yarn. After 32 rotations, pop goes the weasel; the top knob pops up. The farmhouse also displayed a wreath made from human hair. A very pleasant Mormon sister gave me a private tour. She told me the site was once all desert. But that didn't bother me because this desert was still visible.

**Mark Twain, Roughing It (Hartford: American Publishing Company, 1892) at Chapter 14.
***J.W. Powell, The Exploration of the Colorado River and its Canyons (New York: Dover Press, 1985).

China and the USA are a lot alike except Where's Waldo seems different.

17
The Other Side of the World

I went to China and had a great trip. This was especially pleasing because I was sick and tired of people asking me—why are you going there? China is a huge country with a long history. The book *merely summarizing* Chinese history had 757 pages. For much of recent history, most people on earth have lived in China. Why not visit China? It was a challenging destination. Listening to language tapes, it took me three months just to recognize the five tones. Other than Jackie Chan's subtitled movies, I hadn't had much interaction with anything Chinese since my college days. Maybe it was an odd choice for me.

    I had not tried much Chinese food before this trip, so during my first few days, I went to breakfast buffets and tried all the offerings to better recognize the types of foods. There were crunchy vegetables, coleslaw type dishes, greasy pickle slices, and usually celery slices marinated with onion. I wasn't partial to the spongy dumplings or the sticky rice offerings. I wore my fleece jacket to breakfast. After I put it on the back of the chair, an attendant covered it with a green nylon slipcover. I had seen them do this to a man's suit coat. I was impressed that my fleece rated the same attention. My table was in front of a black and white framed photograph of a river scene with a man in a boat seemingly fishing out a dragon!

    I did like some of the dumplings, especially the ones from a street vendor that had the consistency of a crumpet and were filled with a Swedish meatball mixture. Another good street vendor treat was the morning snacks, which were a thick round of fried dough with bits of spicy sausage cooked into it. I also found many meat pie bakeries. I had always associated meat pies with England. Did the English get them from China? In addition to the fried scorpion and snake, there was chicken. But the chicken seemed like an odd dish at times, particularly when you found a blackened chicken's foot or rounds of chicken neck. The street vendors sold baked sweet potatoes so I was never starving. When I was in Nepal, I learned that a lot of people think that Chinese food is the best: the saying goes like this: a lucky man eats Chinese food, has a Japanese wife, and lives in the U.S.A.

There are certain rules for touring in China. You need to stay at fairly nice hotels. Other places will tell you they have no vacancies. People don't seem to mind cutting in line here. In fact, I was frequently advised to push in front by people seeing me getting trampled. When I entered a public garden, a guard would frequently escort me out to a ticket booth and then call someone to work at the booth where I would purchase a ticket with pretty pictures on it so I could walk about the park. If you looked Asian, you didn't seem to need a ticket. In one garden, four tables of old men were playing *Mah Jongg* for many onlookers. Even more entertaining were the fabulous acrobatic shows, which included jumping through hoops, balancing on their hands on successively stacked chairs, standing eight on a bicycle, doing contortions...you name it. When a show ended, I would think, "I am so glad I didn't miss that." I seemed to find the best shows when traveling by foot.

My flight from Shanghai to Beijing has faded from my memory. But I do recall that after collecting my luggage, I set forth to take the local bus to my hotel. Having been lost on the Shanghai subway the night before, I was a bit wary so I stopped at the information booth for reassurance. The two young women there agreed it should be easy to get to my hotel by bus. My directions said to get off at the last stop on the bus route and then walk toward the train station. At the last stop, the bus emptied out and drove away. I seemed to be on the outskirts of a college campus. I didn't see any train station. I asked passers-by where it was, in my best Chinese. Nobody knew. A student took some time to help me. I learned from him they had added three more stops to the bus route but my directions would have worked a month earlier. That explained the lack of any nearby train station. The student suggested I take a taxi. That sounded do-able. I thanked him and started to flag down a taxi.

In fact, I flagged down several taxis only to have others charge in front of me to get in the slowing taxi before it stopped for me. After a full hour of this frustration, one driver turned out the interlopers, insisting I had been there first. I showed the driver my hotel information; he crinkled his nose as he stared at it. When he returned it to me, I got in the taxi with my bag. I felt sure this glitch would soon be over. After about 20 minutes, the driver pulled over and got out of the taxi. He went into a shop for a minute and then returned and we drove off again. (My Chinese wasn't good enough for small talk so I just assumed we were passing a shop he had business in anyway.) After about 5-10 minutes, he pulled into an intersection crowded with pedestrians. He pulled over and got out of the taxi. I saw him approach a young woman who was walking on the crowded sidewalk. After speaking with her, the driver came back to the taxi and told me he could not take me to my hotel. That is the only part I understood. (I gave him some money as he did drive me around a long while and was very pleasant and if it weren't for him, I still might have been trying to flag down a taxi.) The young woman, with whom he had spoken, came over to me. She spoke some English and explained I was very far from my hotel, but gave me directions by bus and pointed me toward the bus station.

I set off so glad my bag had internal straps enabling me to convert it to a backpack. The bus station was mobbed. I managed to find and board the right bus. I had notes in small enough denomination so as not to upset the ticket seller on board and I asked for his help in recognizing my next stop as my directions were to transfer to another bus route at some point. I found my stop and got off the first bus to catch my second bus, but there was no second bus. The many people, who had poured out of the first bus with me, were quickly disappearing so I set off in the direction where the majority seemed to have gone. I was on dusty, dirt roads with no shops or signs within sight. It was getting toward late afternoon. I found some people chatting by the roadside, but with my "broken" Chinese, they didn't want anything to do with me. After a while, I came to a paved street and saw a few standing taxis. Through my few vocabulary words, my hotel information and some pantomime, the drivers understood enough to give me directions to the next bus stop, a short walk away.

This bus stop was adjacent to an industrial building that looked like a factory. The senior citizens, who were waiting there for their bus, turned toward me while I tried to ask about which bus routes stopped there. Once I paused, they briefly grinned at me and turned back to their own conversations. I just had to wait and see what bus came along. The third bus to arrive was the transfer route in my bus directions! I got on. The ticket seller on board the bus looked tired and I was afraid he wasn't going to help me. But I stressed to him that I was long lost and needed to find a particular train station (where I should have been after taking the airport bus). I think my "I am lost" was spoken correctly and loudly enough to get his attention. (I remember learning that phrase and thinking—-what a thing <u>not</u> to say while in a foreign country. But it proved useful.) The ticket seller did nod in my direction when we reached the bus stop next to my long sought train station. I got off the bus. It was dark. I must have had a lost look still because after a minute of walking toward the train station, a businesswoman, also walking on the sidewalk, stopped and asked me if I needed help. I showed her my hotel information. She took her cell phone out of her briefcase and called the hotel and then gave me directions in English. That was my first day in Beijing.

I learned that cats are not part of the Chinese zodiac because the rat forgot to wake up the cat when the zodiac signs were being designated; this is also why cats chase rats. There were no rats to be found on the city streets. City streets in Beijing and Shanghai and most everywhere else were very clean. Maintenance workers swept the streets with brooms. I think workers were assigned to specific street blocks rather than rotating throughout a city. Perhaps that personal responsibility for a visible section of road encouraged such fine service. Unlike the streets, public toilets could be horrendous. Sometimes, there were partially open stalls with a hole in the floor and no toilet paper or sink. One train station had only a shallow dry trough all along a big empty room. These shortcomings in places where I expect indoor plumbing always seemed to rattle me more than they should. But even cats expect kitty litter.

Then there were turtles, and I didn't learn why they weren't part of the Chinese zodiac. There were even turtles with dragon heads at the Forbidden City. Constructed between 1406 and 1420, it was "forbidden" because commoners couldn't enter and hope to leave alive. I was thinking this would be the wrong time to step through a time portal as I entered beyond the inner gate. First was the palace area where the Emperor had resided. Perhaps for show or maybe to keep him from getting lonely, the Emperor resided with 10,000 ladies-in-waiting, 9,000 eunuchs, 3,000 concubines, the Empress, and the Emperor's children. I met an art student there who spoke excellent English; he was going to an art show in Manchester, England as an interpreter for his teacher. He talked about traditional artwork and explained that the higher the contrast, the better the work, and that the ink should not bleed through the paper. It was good to talk to someone I could understand at a place that prompted so many questions. I forgot to ask why the turtle with the dragon's head symbolized the longevity of the emperor.

Si Ma Tai, the "most dangerous part" of the Great Wall of China, was about a two-hour drive from Beijing. I climbed to the fifth tower on a gorgeous blue-sky day. Looking out from the tower, I could imagine a soldier spotting an intruder miles away. The Great Wall at Si Ma Tai was built between 1368 and 1644 and was very steep in places with narrow steps slanting downward. Fortunately, a local hawker held my hand on the scarier places. That was well worth buying the picture book from her when I reached the parking lot. The book included a certificate that read: "Not a plucky hero until one reaches the Great Wall." I learned from another tourist that seven days later, a blizzard had blown in from Siberia, which meant he made it only to the first tower and couldn't see much of anything. I felt lucky.

The Pearl Market in Beijing was on the second floor of a huge retail building. I rode the escalator up and found a shop full of pearls that looked like a wholesale shop. As I went in, a saleswoman was asking a Western man how much he was interested in spending and he said, "Ten thousand U.S. dollars." I looked for a long time as I assumed that is all I would do and it had been a long journey getting there. There were bundles of strung pearls in boxes sorted by quality. These were fresh water pearls, and I was told that the strands of round and evenly sized pearls were the best. There were white, ivory, and cream pearls. The sales people held up different shades and opined as to which color went with my skin color. I picked out a line of creamy small pearls. I watched them string them; tying a knot between each pearl. I bet that man spending a mint doesn't wear his pearls as much as I wear mine.

One of my favorite places was the historic city of Xian (pronounced s*he-yawn*). The city had been the capital of China for 2,000 years. In the Bell Tower—in addition to a big bell—a group of musicians in traditional costume played traditional instruments. Watching them, I felt like I had stepped back in time, but then I looked out the window. Looking down from the Bell Tower, you had a great view of the city full of colorful cars on wide, straight streets. The traffic lights had meters showing the seconds left before a light turned red like some of the pedestrian traffic lights in the U.S.A. (I found that very futuristic for an historic place.)

I walked about the Muslim Quarter. The mosque, built in 742 A.D., had dragons adorning its stonework. The Muslims settled here because this is the beginning of the Silk Road. At the market, I bought a long painted brass fingernail that I could wear like a finger pick. (The Empress dowager Cixi [pronounced *she-she*] had worn one on each finger in her court portrait and she had ruled China starting around 1858 for 50 years while she had the prince imprisoned so he couldn't take the throne.) Supper in the Muslim Quarter featured pork bits served on wheel spokes. Also offered were sheep intestines served on wheel spokes, but they were very greasy. After dinner, at the night market, I shopped at the local wig stall and tried on all sorts of colors and styles. I finally settled on bangs; I haven't had those since third grade. I was just about deciding on black locks with frosted highlights when I noticed a local crowd of about

50 people had encircled me, watching me try on wigs. I purchased the short red hairdo that was in my hand and stepped out of the limelight.

There is a tall pagoda in Xian where they store the translations of Buddhist texts brought from India to China by a Chinese monk. It is called the Wild Goose Pagoda because the monks were looking to eat, and no meat was to be found until a flock of geese flew overhead. They killed one and had goose to eat. The monks took the fallen goose as a sign from Buddha, and thus the pagoda was built on that spot to house the translations. Near the pagoda, I took a guided tour of an art museum. Copies of paintings found in tombs from the Tang Dynasty (618–907 A.D.) were big and colorful. One painting showed a group of women with beehive hairdos that were very 1960s U.S.A. and with dresses with long sleeves that looked Japanese. One of the women held a rooster and was described as a palace courtesan working the cock fights. Another painting showed five cows; the emperor wanted a scholar to come to court so the scholar sent this painting to the emperor. We were told the emperor then knew why the scholar did not want to come to court because the first cow had reins, while the shabbier cows at the end of the line-up were free to ramble. (I thought it was very smart of the emperor to see that.) Another painting showed three visitors (a Roman, a Japanese, and a Han) being received at the Tang Court. The guide told us you could tell the Roman by his big nose. Another room was filled with "farmers' art" spurred by the Cultural Revolution. These paintings of farm animals and of fields were all in bright colors with no open space on the page. Also near the Wild Goose Pagoda, was a history museum with a Double Six Magic Square, a tablet to be buried in a house foundation to ward off evil. The numbers in each line were said to add up to 111 whether counted horizontally, vertically or diagonally.

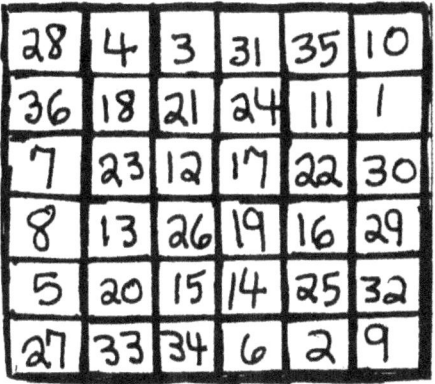
Double Six Magic Square

Still in Xian, customers could pose for photos at a factory making replicas of the terracotta warriors. Photographs were not allowed at the historical site with the unburied terracotta warriors found in the emperor's tomb. Those warriors are life-sized and were made for the tomb of the first emperor of China who died in 200 B.C. (It is said that this emperor, Qin Shihuang, established a written language, monetary currency, a system of measurements, and a network of roads and canals.) His tomb lay buried for more than 2,000 years and only was discovered in 1974 by farmers when they were digging a well. The tomb site has about 8,000 warriors and horses. The life-sized wooden chariots had fallen apart, but the four terracotta horses posed to pull each chariot were still there. Bits of remaining pigment showed the warriors wore bright blue uniforms. Each warrior has a different face and was positioned to hold weapons that had been long ago removed. There were kneeling archers who strung the bow, and a standing archer who shot the bow so as not to lose time between shots. The general, officer, cavalryman, archer, and warrior each wore a different headpiece, whether it is a hat or a hairstyle, I'm not sure. If I understood correctly, when the general put his hands in front of his stomach so that his right hand was over his left hand, he is giving the signal to attack. Postcards showed the armies up to their waists in dirt before the excavation was completed. This site alone was worth a trip to the other side of the world.

I went with a group to a massage school for the blind. There was a shrine with interesting offerings in the foyer. One offering plate had a dagger stuck in a piece of ginger. We went to the showers and were each given a 2x3 foot towel, which we could keep. After the showers, left only with our towels should we feel any need for the slight modesty they offered, we went to a steam room. From there we were led to a room with a table where we were asked to lie down one at a time to be scrubbed down with a rough sponge. That hurt going over the chest but they didn't speak English, and they were blind so grimaces went unheeded. Then we showered again and were given striped cotton pajamas. Girls got green stripes and boys got blue stripes. We sat in big easy chairs with bright yellow terry cloth backs and were served hot jasmine tea in glasses. As we sipped tea, we were given pedicures (no nail polish). Finally, we were put in rooms with four massage tables in each room. It hurt getting whacked on the head and knuckled on my spine. They pressed so hard on the base of my spine that I was afraid they would break me. But I survived it. We all did. As the students were both blind and didn't speak English, it was inhibiting to say "stop" or "go easy" because you didn't know whether that would be interpreted to mean "harder please."

In Chengdu, I visited the Panda Sanctuary. The Greater Pandas are black and white teddy bears and the Lesser Pandas are brown with striped tails and had the look of big raccoons. Pandas are related to raccoons, in fact. My favorites were the cuddly looking Greater Pandas. They wrestled each other, did somersaults and lazily lounged about. Upon entering the sanctuary, there was a panda stretched out on a bamboo hammock lounging on his back and munching leaves off bamboo branches. His black ears and eye patches gave him a mischievous look. They all had big black paws with long, sharp claws. A panda's lifespan in the sanctuary is about 25 years. They mate for 10 days in the spring while they are between the ages of six and fifteen. Pregnancies last four to six months, and babies stay with the mother for the first year. Generally, only one baby is born at a time. We were told that if a mother has twins in the wild, she abandons one of them. Outside the mating season, pandas are solitary animals. Their reproductive organs were shown in jars. The male's penis is short compared to the female's long vagina. The full skeleton showed the panda has more ribs than a human. Experts estimated that in the year 2000, there were between 500 and 1,000 pandas living in the wild. The panda eat mountain bamboo that is shipped in, not the bamboo that grows in the sanctuary. Pandas like the cold weather but the sanctuary is located in hot Chengdu and acts as the "city's business card." *Chengdu* means "Perfect Metropolis," and it is the capital of the Sichuan Province. China has 21 provinces.

I banged on a huge bell with a gong at a monastery. You ring a bell three times, not just once. The monk guarding the bell seemed disgusted that I didn't know of this protocol. I was at a monastery sitting in front of six larger than life Buddha all with blue hair à la Marge Simpson except not so high. What a scene to ponder. It was at this monastery where I awoke to start my climb of *Emeishan* or Mount Emei. I was photographed for my hiking permit, and my photo was kept electronically in case I got lost on the mountain. It was a fast-paced hike with some fun house features including two narrow suspension bridges each about 35 feet in length. Emeishan is a popular pilgrimage destination for Buddhists. Sometimes, you could see heavyset men in business suits being carried on bamboo seats by pairs of skinny men. There were locals dressed in Sunday clothes walking on the leveler parts. I tried not to moan too much about the climb especially when the old woman with a 5x4 foot bundle of sticks walked down the broken stairs toward me or when porters ran by me with huge bundles of bricks hanging from their shoulders. I had to dodge monkey excrement everywhere. There were big fluffy monkeys that people were feeding and teasing. I kept walking quickly past them because the monkeys looked like they could get dangerous. The mountainside restaurant was outdoors with chickens roaming around. I had freshly killed chicken for supper. The chicken had lots of bones and was cooked with potatoes and ginger and served with egg noodles. Big spiders crawled in the women's restroom at the monastery where I stayed overnight. In the evening, I played poker with Australian tourists who exclaimed regularly "cool bananas." Our card table was round and covered with colorful, inlaid designs. Our seats were matching benches that could be pushed together to make a circle that would fit under the table. The monks started my next day at 4:00 a.m. chanting softly to a light drum. After that, they sang intermittently. Combined with the mountain mist floating upward, it made for a great place for a pilgrimage.

I took a memorable trip down the Yangzi River. Rather than the Three Gorges, however, it was watching *Chicken Run* in Chinese with English subtitles that made a more lasting impression. As we traveled on the river, we would make short stops. At Shibaozhai (which translates as Stone Treasure), we climbed through narrow streets lined with vendors on our way to a red wooden pagoda. One butcher's stall had a plate of long pig tails and another had cooked whole rabbits with their long ears. A man walked by carrying two live chickens by their ankles. We passed by people playing *Mah Jongg* on crowded tables in a dark tearoom. After climbing many sets of wooden steep steps, we reached the pagoda with colorful life-sized statues and art work. There was a golden dragon on the corner of the roof that looked like it was in flight. From the pagoda, we had excellent views of the farmland scheduled for flooding by the dam in 2009. Wherever we stopped at a dock, we faced hundreds of winding steps leading uphill into the town. In fact, tramping up and down never-ending steps was a recurring exercise throughout my journey in China.

Heavy construction work is done by hand in China. Workers pried stone out of the ground, broke the stones into little pieces, and then carried it over to a truck for loading. Workers used pieces of wood to hand chisel indentations in the steps and paths and walls. The government could buy a few bulldozers, but that would put a whole lot of people out of work. Most people in China have government-assigned jobs, and many wore the snappy looking uniforms provided. A uniform does a lot toward clothing people, and many people find self-esteem in a uniform. I saw many rural people wearing Mao uniforms of blue or at least wearing the blue Mao caps. He kept popping up. A huge statue of Mao atop a high building waved at the world going by. We stopped at a farmhouse for lunch and the walls were full of pictures of Chairman Mao. In some houses, there would be shrines to Mao. Coming from the west, I found this very odd. One person put it this way: "My grandfather and my father say—with Chairman Mao, every man has a foot." (I think that means they aren't kneeling.) A tourist asked if all Chinese leaders were addressed as Mao! (For the record, that tourist was not from the U.S.A.)

In Yangshuo, I went on a night tour to watch cormorant fishing. By the boat's lantern, we saw five cormorants (tall black birds) preen and then jump in the water and glide about in search of fish. The fisherman kept a string around the neck of each bird. The string prevented the bird from devouring the fish, I think. After the bird caught some fish, the man would pull in the bird by the string and take the bird by the neck and shake it upside down over a straw basket until the bird coughed up the fish. They were slender fish about six inches long. He fed seven fish to a cormorant and then tipped it upside down and shook it until the seven fish were "coughed" into the basket. Then, he gave that bird a fish to actually eat. I'm not sure what I witnessed was quite a humane practice, but the birds looked beautiful; they seemed healthy and well kept. After a long swim, the bird would shake off (beat its wings at a rapid pace) so that its breast feathers looked dry. It's hard to tell with birds, but they looked satisfied with the arrangement.

Bicycling through the country mountainside in Yangshuo, many ducks and water buffalo animated the scenery. The guide, Andy, spoke great English. He went to school until age 14 and learned some English there. The rest he picked up from tourists and U.S.A. movies. He was one of the few guides I met who I could understand well. Travelling along dirt roads and paths between fields and ponds, he never rushed me. Andy said the farmlands were owned by farm families but seemed surprised when I asked if the pathways we traveled were public; they were. Rice was spread out on rooftops to dry. At one stop, a farmer shaved a stick of sugarcane and cut it in one-inch rounds. You chewed this round of sugarcane for the juice and then spit out the pulp. (It had the consistency of celery, but it was harder, much like a hard apple.) At Andy's house, his mother peeled us a *pomolo,* a huge grapefruit type fruit shaped more like a pear. You opened the skin of each section to remove the seeds before eating the fruit. His mother had pomolo skins set out on her roof to dry that Andy said she would use to make medicine. Whenever it was time to start bicycling again, Andy would say: "It's time to rock and roll." After a full morning, to return to the starting point, we bicycled a bit on the paved roads. It amazed me that the weaving cars and trucks seemed less intimidating on a bicycle than from a bus. I think that was because I was doing the driving.

In Leshan, I took a ferry across the river to see the Grand Buddha or *Da Fo*. The ferry rules were posted at the dock. The most thought-provoking were: "Don't set sail for the boats that are broken or have no complete driving instruments" and "Keep the deformed, sick and drunk crew off driving boat." After a short ride to the far side of the river, you debark at the bottom of a path leading upward to the top of the Da Fo steps. Along the path was rock ledge and at one point, a dragon was sculpted onto the ledge. The dragon looked to be in a perpetual shower and by the way its paws pushed out of the rock, it looked like the dragon was enjoying the shower. This was my favorite of all the dragons I encountered in China, and there were many. At the top of the path, I was on level with the Da Fo head and his whole body was 233 feet tall. This Buddha sat on the side of a cliff by the river. I was distracted from the head by the other people milling around at the top of the path. People were buying caged birds to set them free. People were buying padlocks to fasten onto one of the many nearby ropes and then throw away the key. Because it was a Buddha, it was a worshipping spot for many so these acts probably had some religious significance. Looking back at the Buddha's face, I realized that I was smaller than its ear, and its face looked grim. It gave me pause. I wondered if the giant Buddha had captured that dragon in the rock and rather than enjoying a shower, the dragon was trying to push out of the rock and escape.

    I had started my trip in Shanghai, half way around the world from Boston; it was the same distance whether I traveled east or west. Once I arrived, the hour on my watch was still the same but the afternoon was now the morning. A big statue of Chairman Mao stood near huge plastic flowers in Shanghai. Did that symbolize the One Hundred Flowers in Bloom? A lot of China went uninterpreted for me, so it was no wonder I focused on the dragons. In Shanghai, I watched a parade on Nanjing Donglu. (*Donglu* means street.) What caught my attention is the 20 men, who were dressed in red silk outfits with gold hats, piecing together two 60-foot dragons in preparation for the parade. First, they took out lengths of hoops attached like accordion bellows and they tied those hoop segments together to form a long line. Then, they unfolded a long sheet with a design of beautiful red scales along a gold ridge. They fastened the sheet to the lined-up hoops so by its looks, even I could figure, it must be going to be a dragon. The parade featured a group of uniformed women pushing semi-full shopping carts and a group of uniformed men holding poles bearing posters of various larger-than-life consumer goods. It was either a pro-capitalism parade or a parody on consumerism replacing patriotism. My favorite part was the two red dragons. Dragon in *Chongwen* (Chinese) is *"long,"* the word for snake.

My white porcelain cup with a painted blue dragon says a lot about China. Hot water was always available for tea. In the hotels, the riverboats and the trains, there would be hot water available in a corked thermos. Hotels had the same white porcelain teacups, so I could always make hot chocolate, tea, instant oatmeal, or Chinese noodle soup. Bowls of instant noodles came in three sizes, and it was important to make sure the picture on the bowl didn't have a chili on it unless you tolerate fire like a dragon. Dragons were everywhere—in the architecture, in the interior design, in the dishware...like a *Where's Waldo?* game. Back home, I noticed the dragon's absence more than I had noticed its presence in China. The ever-present silent dragon swirling in the wind had vanished; that seemed the biggest difference between China and the U.S.A.

I went to mainland China in the year 2000 before the U.S.A. became the world's pit bull. China was the place most like the United States that I have ever visited. Why? All of the people over a vast expanse of land spoke the same language, used the same currency and had the same national politicians and local practices. As a foreign tourist in China, I was ever reminded of foreign tourists in the U.S.A. in similar situations. When I was lost on a bus with a bunch of senior citizens who didn't want to bother to understand my accent, I thought this might happen to a Chinese tourist in New England. The Shanghai Museum's comment on minority cultures in China even reminded me of home: "Our splendid and glorious Chinese civilization is the result of the assimilation of various nationalities that have lived in China." It was a melting pot, but you had to squint to see beyond the uniformity. Just like in the U.S.A., the majority of people seemed secure in their belief that their country was strong and a power to be reckoned with. (But there, newspaper pages were posted in common areas with articles to reinforce this "patriotism.") Maybe it was just the badminton. Lots of people played badminton there, and I like badminton. That might be why I found it so reminiscent of home.

Three weeks in Australia made quite an impression, at least the insects and the reptiles did. They were visible where they should not be and invisible where you knew they were.

18
And the Kangaroo Danced to the Didjeridu

In a frame against gold matte is a whimsical wallaby set in a sea of red. In the corner is my painted *didjeridu* (a traditional instrument) that makes me smile whenever I catch a glimpse of it. If for no other reason, these two pieces keep my short trip to Australia on my mind. Australia is a continent about the size of the U.S.A., and I only had three weeks to see some bit of it. Other than hoping to see a kangaroo, I had no set expectations. I spent a week wandering about the City of Sydney and then joined a two-week camping tour in the Northern Territory, which occupies about one-sixth of Australia's land mass. Sydney had much more of a Southeast Asian feel than I had anticipated, but that isn't why it's on my mind.

In Sydney, the airport van dropped me off a block away from my lodging, which was at the end of a one-way street. After the long journey and lugging my bag the last block, I was glad to arrive. But as I put away my luggage, I observed big brown insects here and there in the room. Feeling sure they were cockroaches, I decided not to nap quite yet and set off to see what other options might be nearby. On the street, I noted I was staying on the same block as the Radisson. That wouldn't be shabby. As I stopped to look at the dresses in the store window, I noted that those same brown insects were climbing and resting on the manikins. Ooh. I mentioned it to a passerby who calmly commented that it was a moth explosion. It seems I landed in the city on the first day of this phenomenon, which explained why there was nothing in the news about it. I stayed with my initial lodging. When I pulled the curtains at night, at least five of them fell on my head resulting in much shrieking and twitching on my part. The next day, there was still nothing in the news, and people appeared very nonchalant about the condition. Riding up an escalator, one of these huge moths landed with a thud on the well-dressed woman in front of me. She didn't bat an eye. If this had been Boston, people would have been in hysterics. In fact, on the third day, a clerk pointed out that I had one on my shoulder. I jumped; I screamed; the clerk smiled in awkward surprise. The moths would flutter about and cluster while I wandered in museums. It confounded me that I seemed to be the only one jumping and gasping when the moths swarmed en masse about people's heads. I thought they were taking the whole "explosion" far too much in stride. That is my biggest impression of Sydney.

From visiting Sydney with the brown moths, I took a plane to the Northern Territory, a place inhabited by silently still lizards. Like the moths, they would often appear and cause no apparent commotion, prompting the sensation that creatures were taking liberties with my reality. It was a hot camping excursion; the first week was in a desert with nose-bleeding dry heat, and the second week was in tropics with sauna conditions (before and after showering felt so much the same that there was no need for a towel in between). Travelling in the dry season, we saw canyons up to 100 feet steep, which we were told would fill with water in the wet season. The guide's stories of early European explorers provided a welcome distraction to the heat. The explorers who set off in the wet season drew maps showing vast stretches of water; very unlike the maps drawn by those who set off in the dry season. So explorers could blame the map when, as frequently happened, they exhausted their supplies, ended up eating their transportation (horses or camels) and found themselves in a barren place that didn't believe in coddling its visitors. I hoped they had brought head nets to deal with the persistent, darting flies. A rescue party found one explorer just three days after he had caught and eaten a whole baby wallaby, fur and all. (He later said it was the best thing he had ever eaten!)

Another expedition was about to call it quits being marooned in the wet season. When Sunday came around, the leader read the Bible for a Sunday service, and the biblical passage talked about crossing the water on animal skins. He had his crew recover the skins of the horses they had already eaten, and they somehow fashioned a boat with the horse skins and escaped. We weren't lost, but I could still empathize with the plight of those early explorers. (I could imagine as I had driven, in fact, around Santa Cruz for hours on end trying to find a road without an abrupt end on a day after a hurricane had washed out most of its bridges.) Back in the Northwest Territory, I lost count of the junked vehicles strewn along the desolate main highway. And I became more certain that joining a tour was the better way to see this part of the world.

From the highway, I could see solitary camels wandering on the desert landscape. The guide said they were brought over from the Middle East in the late 1800s for transportation. Imported food accompanied them but they would have none of it and trotted off fully content with their new desert environs. They say, cattle rustlers round up the camels to sell in the Middle East and can do so because the camels are considered feral. While the camel remains unprotected because it is an introduced animal, the cattle grass is protected even though it is an introduced grass. The thriving cattle grass was destroying my illusion of a red rock interior, and I learned it is an imported plant for cattle feed. (The kangaroos try to avoid it.) A local caterpillar would reportedly eat it up, but the government won't let the caterpillar lose on it because the cattle industry exerts sufficient political pressure against the notion that the cattle grass is a weed to be eradicated. Life is full of contradictions.

But at least the tourist industry seems to have seen to it that the kangaroos and crocodiles are still there. In the north, crocodile warnings were posted along the road. We were told that a crocodile had attacked three men a while back and killed one, whereas the other two climbed a tree to escape. Rather than eat its victim, the crocodile just waved the corpse at the two in the tree keeping them stranded for some time. It was explained that this was a "territorial display" on the crocodile's part and served to reinforce my notion that crocodiles are dead serious about property rights.

At the Tenant Creek Mining Museum, the admission ticket was a certificate authenticating our mining rights on the property. (There was no mention as to crocodiles' respect for such certificates.) In 1936, gold was discovered in the granite at Tenant Creek attracting miners to the area. There was gold but no water so that convoy trucks would bring in 40 tons of food and 80 tons of beer. People would hang their beer in a wet woolen sock to cool it. A letter of advice to those charged with recruiting miners said to forget looking for the best men for the job and instead interview the wives. If the wife couldn't tolerate living without amenities, the man would leave within months. (Given that the mining involved banging hard rock with hand tools, I thought some of those men may have been using their wives as an excuse to quit.) There were few women and children in Tenant Creek even into the 1940s, but the museum highlighted its story through the eyes of a miner's young son. It told how he had lost contact with his childhood friend because indigenous people weren't allowed on the land after mining rights were issued. The museum said that "Freedom, Fortitude and Flies" summed up the day and age after gold was discovered. I could understand the fortitude and the flies, but it wasn't until the young son described returning to Tenant Creek in the 1950s after water pipes had been routed into the town that I understood the freedom. He said that he stopped in the bar for a drink as had always been his routine, and a young police officer told him to get out because he was too young. He left and was hoping the officer didn't notice that he was driving off in a car. I recognized the freedom lost. And I recall thinking that a moth explosion would likely be taken in stride in Tenant Creek.

Continuing north, I encountered kangaroos and wallabies and emus and many bats. The fruit bats hung in trees by the hundreds. They were big and black and made a lot of noise when they flapped their wings. Hundreds in the sky were a spectacle, but meeting up with one on your own late at night while watching for snakes on your way to the outhouse was very unnerving. The wallabies reminded me of large rats when they put their noses to the ground. The emus were officious characters strutting up and down. The kangaroos retained an otherworldly look. The surroundings were not to be outdone by the creatures. It was sometimes rocky desert, sometimes palm trees, sometimes canyons, sometimes rows of termite mounds looking like cemetery markers, sometimes huge rocks...If you looked at my photos, you would see that I liked the rocks. In climbing and sliding around some of the huge red boulders, it is fair to say I encountered some anxiety as well. But not all the rock involved climbing.

Some of the rock had what looked like colorful but weathered graffiti that was called "rock art." The art could not be carbon dated, but it was said that some rock art sites started 40,000 years ago based on archeological excavations at the sites. A guide explained that the painting on the rock was done with ochre, a long-lasting paint that permeated the rock. To demonstrate, he wet a piece of ochre and used it to paint red around his wrist. He then showed us that while he was able to wash off his outer skin, the red paint had already sunk below the skin surface. We were told that up until the 1960s, the indigenous peoples painted traditional paintings over older paintings. Given this background, I never had a good sense of whether I was viewing artwork that was rendered in contemporary or olden times. We were told indigenous people traditionally used their hand print for their signature, and many hand prints were rendered in colorful ochre on the rock. There was also a good deal of serpent imagery; we were told the squiggly lines on the rock represented the rainbow serpent from creation stories. At Nourlangie Rock, there was a figure outlined in white paint and described as an evil spirit who eats women after hitting them with a yam. (I thought that was a curious spirit; another visitor commented that yams must have been plentiful.) And who, exactly, were these people who had painted these figures, these kangaroos, water lilies, and evil spirits on the rock?

These were people living in Australia at the time of Captain Cook's 1770 discovery (his discovery of Australia or Australia's discovery of Captain Cook). Many different cultural groups lived in Australia at that time. Most of these groups are still there but now live in government settlements that aren't separated by culture. We were told, however, that residents of these settlements still retain an identity with their individual clan and are careful to check with the leaders of any different clan prior to entering onto that other clan's traditional territory. Whatever their clan, they are generally referred to as Australian aboriginals. The government started a program in the 1970s under which aboriginal peoples could apply for the return of property rights. The Joweyn, one of the indigenous groups, petitioned for land rights in 1978 but only obtained land rights in 1989. A Joweyn elder was relating that the government didn't want to return Katherine Gorge to his community because "they said we would take it away from everyone." He concluded, "I don't know where we were supposed to take it to, but it is still here." I saw it; it is still there.

It seemed as if the Australian aboriginal peoples were frequently highlighted in Australia while at the same time, they remained ever un-present. Museum exhibits talked about aboriginal creation stories and secret laws; there were men's laws and women's laws, and only those deemed capable of using the laws were instructed in them. One exhibit said that traditional law held that a man accused of murder would be given a shield and then the relatives of the victim were permitted to throw spears at the accused. In another museum, it spoke of aboriginal men being proud of their ability to fend off spears with a shield. I didn't have any opportunities to visit aboriginal communities in the Northern Territory but did attend a presentation on the traditional weapons and implements used to survive in the bush. We were told that while the emu has a tender neck, it is better to aim a boomerang for the leg so that you can catch the emu. We were also shown "bush tucker" or the various plants and insects you could gather in the bush for sustenance. (The dried chunk of sap called a desert lollipop looked like it could be tasty.)

The event calendars were not filled with didjeridu concerts. In fact, the only advertisement I saw for a didjeridu show was a concert to be performed by a Swede. (As it turned out, he had spent 27 years working in land management in the Northern Territory and was quite well versed in the instrument.) He had an assortment of didjeridus and used different lengths for different songs. His were painted in colorful design like mine. (I saw locals using unpainted ones that they dipped in the water before playing.) The didjeridu is a hollowed out, straight branch with a circumference of approximately two inches with the hollowed portion having a circumference of about one inch; melted wax lines the "mouthpiece." It is generally four to five feet long and the surface is smooth. To play the didjeridu, you blow into it to make a deep, bellowing sort of sound. I got my didjeridu in an artisan's shop. I encountered aboriginal artwork in the tourist shops, but I saw no aboriginal neighborhoods or restaurants. This "visible but not present" status seemed to be a continuing trend as the earliest European census of Sydney counted no aboriginals, but contemporaneous paintings and writings indicate they were there.

Through guide narratives and museum markers, one could glean tidbits of a turbulent history. An artist's description of a painting talked of aborigines being chased and beaten by white farmers after the aborigines quit working in response to the nonpayment of wages. In the town of Battle Creek, aboriginal people had attacked the telegraph outpost, leaving two telegraph workers dead. In response, government forces carried out much more deadly attacks in retaliation against the aborigines. At one time, aboriginal groups took up arms against ranchers who homesteaded a cattle ranch near King's Canyon atop a community water hole reserved for the dry season; again the government retaliation was much more deadly. Some European explorers tortured the locals for information on the whereabouts of water and some sought their help.

At Escape Cliff, we were told about two European explorers who found themselves at a distance from their rifles as a group of aborigines approached, shouting and shaking spears at them. These unarmed men needed to distract their attackers before being speared so they started to waltz. The menacing group just stared at them while the two men waltzed over to their rifles, fired some shots in the air and ran. Other stories told of aboriginal groups harboring lost European explorers while they waited for a European rescue party to happen along.

In addition to this sometime turbulent history, the Australian Prime Minister had just imposed some severe measures against alcoholic beverages in aboriginal communities. From the very beginning of my camping trip, I noticed stacks of red postcards in every bar warning of these new restrictions on alcohol. Editorials and letters to the editors were still weighing in on the matter. There seemed to be many complications in several directions. Aboriginal people are paid "sit down money" by the government. (If I understood correctly, that is so they don't roam the land throwing spears at kangaroos and such). Every so often, I saw a political poster that declared: "No more sit down money." Albert Namatjira, a famous watercolor artist, was the first aborigine to be given citizen status in Australia and that was just in the late 1950s. Providing alcohol to aborigines was illegal, but as a citizen, Mr. Namatjira could buy alcohol. Under his community laws, he was bound to share with his neighbors. As such, this first aboriginal citizen was jailed for offering his neighbors a drink.

From the early 1900s to the 1970s, the government routinely removed aboriginal children from their parents as an "altruistic" measure so they wouldn't grow up tainted by connections with the "dying" aboriginal cultures; some testimonials related that growing up in the white world was a lucky happenstance that gave them better job opportunities, but the majority of these removed children related less than satisfactory childhoods. Most grew up in environments in which they were confronted with constant reminders that they didn't fit in. And as everyone knows, a shot and a chaser can help make you feel at home. But those red postcards warned that you can't have a drink anywhere inside an aboriginal community. "Aboriginal community" sounded like a misnomer; aborigines were abundantly present in the towns where these bars were selling drinks. Granted, I sensed some dissonance about the aborigines' presence in the towns. For example, the aborigines might be sitting in a large group in the middle of a traffic island while the whites drove on the roads or walked on the sidewalks. But both groups were there, in the same location.

To these tourist eyes, there seemed to be parallel worlds for the whites and aborigines even sharing the same sidewalk. I sat down for a coffee and pastry at a dismal sidewalk one hot morning. I did so because a man on the sidewalk was playing Roger Miller songs on a guitar and rendering them with a sweet, husky voice. About two sips into my coffee, the cafe owner turned on some elevator music of dubious audio quality. I wondered if he had a clue that the street singer, an aboriginal man, was probably the only good reason to stop at this end of the sidewalk. There appeared to be a deep divide even while nothing was said about it. Being from New England, I am accustomed to these unspoken, deep divides. I remember being on a bus somewhere around Portland, Oregon, and eavesdropping on a local showing the city to a visitor. The visitor asked, "So what kind of people live out here mostly?" The local said, "Mostly whites." The visitor asked, "But what are they?" The local said, "I don't know; they're just whites." I understood the visitor, but I still have no clue what either group of Australians understands.

Nonetheless, the journey was a learning experience. I learned that traditional fishing was done with a spear instead of a hook so that rather than wait for feeding fish to bite the bait, you could spear sleeping fish unawares. No mention was made, however, regarding how one might know where the fish sleep. With all my swimming in beer trying to beat the heat though, perhaps I should have just tried thinking like a fish to find them sleeping. I'm still trying to identify what looked like a large bluewinged kangaroo; at least that is what I could have sworn

I saw one night. Or was the kangaroo pole-vaulting using a didjeridu?

Coming home to New England after two weeks of camping with lizards and watching for the snakes, I found myself studying the autumn leaves covering the sidewalk to avoid inadvertently stepping on a snake that might likely be poisonous. (What was I thinking?) Australia has its own ways of staying with you even after you leave.

Eastern Europe provided a sideways look into gulags and accented the historical violations of people's right to liberty.

19
Mushrooming Anxiety

With all the war zones and the hostility toward the U.S.A., the former Soviet satellites north of Vienna seemed one of the safer places to visit. On the one hand, it sounded like a destination that could wait for my retirement; on the other hand, there was the Cyrillic alphabet to tackle. Ultimately, it was with enthusiastic anticipation that I studied Russian to prepare for this opportunity to see the churches, the art museums, and the architecture. My itinerary started in St. Petersburg, Russia, and slowly wound its way through adjacent countries that mostly offered menus written in Russian too.

The czar, Peter the Great, designated St. Petersburg as Russia's capital in 1703. Like Washington DC, it is a relatively new capital, which was built on a swamp and is packed with beautiful architecture. And, just like DC, the subways are excellent. Escalators in the subways were speedy, but traveled so far that it easily took three minutes to get to the train platform. It made me think about what it might be like if one of those moving stairways suddenly broke down. Then I felt irritated that all the travel warnings must be making me paranoid.

In St. Petersburg, I was staying at a hostel that offered transportation from the airport. Nobody was waiting for me at the airport. I exchanged some dollars for Rubles and purchased a phone card so I could call to inquire. But I couldn't figure out how to use the card with the public pay phone. The woman, who had sold me the card, gave me an intimidating look and turned away when I asked her for help. Luckily my transport arrived by then, and we drove off to inch through a never-ending traffic jam. Once at the hostel, I learned that a city walking tour would start from there the next morning. I signed up for the tour and went to bed, hopeful that the next day would be better.

Our walking tour guide, Nicholas, took us to an open food market where food was sold from stalls. The merchants plied you with samples if you looked even remotely interested. I stopped to check out the pickle stands and was assailed by aggressive vendors giving me multiple samples of pickled you name it. One sample was even pickled stems of garlic clusters. The honey vendors were adamant that I try their samples even though I kept trying to break away. The buckwheat honey was extremely strong, and I was hoping I could keep it down. The rabbits in the meat case had a single furry foot. Nicholas noted that this was to show it is truly a rabbit and not a cat!

Many of the church buildings we passed housed museums or government organizations. Nicholas said that churches died out and were converted to warehouses or museums or for other uses because of poor church attendance. Priests worked for the KGB (the Soviet secret police), and those who refused were shot dead. The secret police were brutal under Stalin. Nicholas explained that Stalin started to systematically eliminate the other revolutionaries, because they knew he was a "nobody" in the Revolution, but the common people didn't know that. I had asked Nicholas to point out the hammer and sickle insignia on buildings from the Soviet era. He showed us an apartment building with a hammer and sickle; it seemed more like a coat of arms. He said that this insignia on a building would signify that all the residents of that building were watching for bad conduct and had pledged to report any observations of bad conduct to the KGB. We Westerners, with our notions of a nefarious KGB, were much appalled at this fact, so he explained that such conduct was viewed as patriotic. Nicholas said, too, that in Russian history, the poor had lived separated and ignorant lives and along came a government telling them they were important people. Furthermore, the government was willing to help the people fight "the people's enemy." It reminded me of the Boston subway's slogan: "If you see something that is not quite right, report it. If you see something, say something." That sort of thing does make you paranoid about the people's enemy.

We saw a beautiful Empire-style mansion that was yellow with white trim. This prompted Nicholas to tell the story of Rasputin. Rasputin's parents thought he was a visionary because he was able to identify local thieves when he was young. Rasputin studied to be a monk, but he never took his vows. He became an advisor to the Czar because he successfully treated the prince's hemophilia. Rasputin said that he would cure him by the time the prince reached the age of 10. Rasputin also urged the Czar to withdraw from World War I. Another prince, the one who was second in line to the throne, wanted to continue in WWI, so he had Rasputin killed, notably just a month before the hemophiliac prince reached age 10. This rogue prince invited Rasputin to his palace, the yellow mansion with the white trim. First, he gave Rasputin a creamy cake spiked with rat poison, but he didn't die. It was thought that the cream had diluted the poison. Next, they shot him several times, and he ran out of the room. Unfortunately, rather than running out of the palace, he ran toward the inner courtyard. He couldn't scale the courtyard's fence so his killers caught up to him, picked him up, and pushed him through a side door (which we saw), and into a car trunk. Then, they put him in the river under fresh ice. Rasputin's body was found three days later in Helsinki Bay. The autopsy indicated that he died from dehydration or frost bite but not from asphyxiation, not from rat poison, and not from the bullet wounds! We were told these details are known because the prince who had him killed ran to France after the October Revolution and wrote a book giving the details. Nicholas was an excellent tour guide. He said he was going with his father to pick mushrooms the next day.

The next day, I took local bus Number 46 to the Peter and Paul Fort on the Petrovert side of town to visit a museum of Russian life in the late 1800s to early 1900s. Here I saw sketches of a man being publicly whipped and another man being shot by a firing squad and a newspaper article about serfs for sale. I also read a bit about the failure of the December 5th Revolution (the failed 1905 revolt against the autocratic czar), and I wondered if Russia would be a more modern place if the Revolution had succeeded. Another exhibit noted that social distinctions in Russia were based not only on class and wealth but also on dress and appearance. I think that is still happening because the people (male and female) on the street were very well dressed.

The Museum of Political History of Russia was an experience to behold. Upon entering the building, even before purchasing my ticket, I had to put plastic bags over the soles of my shoes. The woman selling me the entry ticket said I needed to check my coat, but the woman at the coat check said my coat was too insignificant to check. I subsequently wandered about the first room looking at fantastic cases displaying very detailed and photographed exhibits of Lenin's rise to power. Then, as I was walking into the second room, the new attendant came bustling over to tell me I needed to check my coat. When I went downstairs again to the coatroom, another woman was on duty and she was unconcerned about my coat's specifics so I was able to check it. Back in the second exhibit room, signs described Stalin's claims that life in the Soviet Union was a piece of cake compared to life outside the Soviet Union. It said that Stalin's fabrications were weakened when World War II troops saw the outside world and could tell it wasn't lagging behind the Soviet Union; instead it was way ahead. Repression thus increased after World War II, and the mock gulag cell for political prisoners looked grim. The Soviet Union's proclamations on "reality" continued, and Stalin portrayed the "enemies of the people" as deformed and otherworldly. The political posters made them look like half donkeys in a vertical line up with the Marx brothers. State propaganda can be scary. As I wandered the displays, I wondered what it must have been like living a lifetime in fear of weapons of mass destruction. I had a lot of time for contemplation as I waited for my bus after touring the museum. After waiting more than an hour for Local Number 46, the bus driver said he wasn't going my way so I took the subway back to downtown St. Petersburg. On the subway, I saw a man with a full basket of mushrooms covered with some freshly picked herbs and thought about the plans Nicholas and his father had to go mushroom picking.

When I visited the Russian Orthodox Church where Dostoyevsky worshipped, a priest was preaching to about 40 people who stood clustered in front of him; there were no pews to be seen. The priest had a long white beard and wore dark blue velvet robes and a matching hat. To me, he looked like a wizard; in particular, the type you see at a modern medieval fair. The far wall was crowded with many framed icons. But the Russian Museum had an even larger exhibit, a wonderful display of religious icons from the 1400s and 1500s.

I bought a postcard of an icon depicting St. George and the Dragon. The vendor at the museum counter was annoyed that I was bothering her to purchase something at her stand even though she didn't seem to be doing anything else. She ignored me despite my protests; I needed her to reach the postcard I wanted. I leaned against the wall contemplating my next move prompting another apathetic attendant to jump to life and berate me for leaning against the wall. I stood at the counter and continued to repeat myself loudly. Eventually, with a glare, she gave me the postcard and took my money. Perhaps it was the cold winters that made the vendor so icy.

At this same museum, a huge painting, almost the height of the wall, showed the Russian Army attacking while sliding down a snowy hillside. Both Napoleon and Hitler tried to conquer St. Petersburg, but they were thwarted by the winter weather. Locals call it "General Frost." One local said something along this line: "We had summer this year but I was working that day." Leaving the museum, it was lightly snowing. I passed a street musician; he was seated on a folding chair playing a musical saw. I walked over to a former KGB building where the lower windows were boarded up. My *Lonely Planet Guide Book* said this was to muffle the screams of the prisoners being tortured. That left me feeling unsettled. I passed the golden arches with McDonald's spelled out in the Cyrillic alphabet, and I knew what it said without sounding it out. After a burger, I felt much more relaxed. It would take more than a horrid sales clerk and a guide book entry to make me forget about the pleasure of listening to that musical saw. I needed more musical entertainment.

Why did my taxi take me to a theater other than the one on my ballet ticket? (For the record, the correct theater was printed on my ticket.) When I gave the usher my ticket to get help finding my seat, she took me to the box office to have the attendant explain in an English word here and there that my ticket was for another place. The usher turned to leave me and I hurried after her. After much frantic effort to communicate and refusing to leave her, she either finally understood or finally agreed to help and fished out the torn off portion of my ticket

Easy reading.

stub. With my two ticket pieces in hand, I raced off to flag a taxi. The taxi drivers were parked in a cluster nearby. I must have been quite a sight (probably bouncing off the sidewalk by that point) because one driver even got out of his taxi to see if he could help me. After looking at my torn ticket, he told me to follow him. We sped off in his taxi. He entered this other theater with me to explain my predicament to the box office. The head honcho walked to the balcony door with me and told the usher to seat me. At intermission, I learned they didn't generally seat people after the curtain was raised but had made an exception for me!

After the show, I decided to walk home and had a lovely walk but had set off in the wrong direction. After a while and after midnight, I stopped at a taxi whose driver was engrossed in a thick novel. When he looked at my hostel card, he quoted a price that sounded expensive. But I was tired and lost so I agreed. About ten minutes later, he stopped as though we had reached my destination. Nothing looked familiar so I told him to drive to the other side of the building. This was not my hostel. I showed him the hostel card again. We drove and then drove some more. About 30 minutes later, between the two of us, we found it. As I left him, he stuck his head out the window and shouted *drew-gah* at me. If I had not taken a Russian language class, who knows what I might have thought when he called me a "friend." It was with mixed emotions that I departed St. Petersburg.

I took the train to Helsinki in Finland or Suomi as the locals call it. (How did we get Finland from Suomi?) Helsinki is a flat city by the sea and has some worthwhile museums. When I stopped for a sandwich at a museum, it was the first time I had experienced a gracious person behind a counter since my Russian adventure began, and I remember feeling stirred by it. It's amazing how little time it takes a person to adjust to callousness such that it is an expected response. In the 1550s, a Swedish King introduced Christianity in Helsinki. St. George was popular in Finland; he was introduced there by Swedish soldiers and invoked to protect livestock against wolves. I got a post card of a wonderful wooden rendering of St. George slaying the dragon. Here, the people selling the postcards acted as if it was what they were being paid to do! An exhibit told of how preachers preached against dressing above one's station in Finland through the 1800s and that 85% of the population is Lutheran. Given my reaction to the vendors, the religion might be helping people go in the right direction. The people on the streets didn't seem as clothes conscious as they had in St. Petersburg. But I would rather admire clothes while window-shopping than while people watching.

At Fort Sveaborg, an historian told of how Finland had been in the midst of war for 850 years prior to 1980, how St. Petersburg was previously part of Finland, and how Helsinki became the capital in 1812. Swedes built the Fort, and its construction took 40 years. During this time, one-tenth of the soldiers died every month from harsh winter conditions and poor food. The duke who planned and oversaw the construction died before it was completed, and the Swedish king designed his burial monument. I thought it looked like a Darth Vadar helmet laid to rest. Wasn't that sort of evil supposed to live in a galaxy far, far away?

I took the ferry across the Gulf of Finland to Tallinn in Estonia. Tallin is the capital, and its buildings from the 1500s make it very quaint. The town gate is lined with cylindrical towers with narrow rectangular windows for the archers; these formed two eyes and a nose. Then, the orange tiled turrets completed the picture of what looked to me like extraterrestrial spies decked out with orange caps positioned to see everything and anything. At the tiny natural history museum, I enjoyed an exhibit on mushrooms; they were categorized as edible, edible after boiling, sometimes poisonous, poisonous, and sometimes fatal. The local beer was A-le-Coq, and light beer in Tallinn (as in the rest of that geographic area) referred to its color rather than the calorie count. Words can be deceiving. From Tallinn, I traveled by train to Riga, the capital of Latvia.

Riga was conquered by Germany in 1210, by Poland in 1561, by Sweden in 1629, by Russia in 1700, and by the Nazis from 1941 to 1944. That last occupation resulted in some Latvians being drafted into the Soviet Army in 1940 and their brothers being drafted into the Nazi army starting in 1941. This would technically have pitted brother against brother in World War II. (What side did their parents root for?) Our guide told us that the Soviet Union "liberated" the free and independent Latvia from capitalism so that it could join the Soviet Union.

At the Latvian Open Air Ethnic Museum, we were told most Latvians had been serfs owned by German or Russian nobility. The old church had a private door in the back that opened to a heated booth for the "owner," who would generally come for the local church service once a month. A metal neck cuff dangled from a vertical board outside the church door, which was reportedly a common punishment in Latvia. They explained if a serf missed service too many times, the authorities would add together a bunch of smaller derelictions to create a more severe charge for which the serf would then be locked in the neck cuff and corporally punished. It was after the service that the congregation was required to stay to watch the corporal punishment being meted out. The church opposed this practice but to no avail. Finally, in 1860, Latvia enacted a law prohibiting the corporal punishment of adults outside the church door. In 1903, serfdom was abolished completely. Latvian is the national language, but 30 percent of the population is Russian. The guide told us Russian children in Latvia go to Russian-speaking schools; he explained Russians are sore about Latvian independence because now Russians applying for jobs and schools are no longer favored just because they are Russians rather than Latvians.

Still in Riga, I attended an opera about a guilt-ridden Lady Macbeth character. She had killed her father-in-law by poisoning his fried mushrooms and her lover killed her husband; they were both thrown into prison. But then I was confused because they were on a ship and kept singing about the cruel guards who seemed to just be minding their own business. The opera was in Russian with subtitles in Russian and in English. So where was Latvian, the official language? After visiting the Occupation Museum, I started to retrace the opera's story. An exhibit explained that Soviet *gulags* (prisons) were mostly located in Siberia or on boats. The prison in the opera had been on a ship. The exhibit explained that the prison guards would incite the prisoners to torment one another and punish any observed kindness between prisoners. In the opera, the guards seemed to escort the boyfriend character a lot. Perhaps they weren't being friendly. The woman, who had killed her husband and father-in-law to be with this boyfriend, was sent to this same prison ship with the boyfriend. This boyfriend seemed to adore her before going to prison. But on the ship, her boyfriend, also a fellow inmate now, betrayed her and repeatedly mocked her, until she jumped overboard. Finally, the opera started to make sense.

Another exhibit at the Occupation Museum said many resistance fighters lived in underground bunkers that were difficult to camouflage in the winter. Movement could shake the snow off tree branches, which would alert KGB spies. Traveling outside the bunker would show footprints in the snow. The exhibit said many resistance fighters were captured when they went home to share a Christmas meal with their families. Furthermore, when the Soviets undertook mass deportations, it was done at night with no prior notice and with no press about it afterwards. The movie on the bus to Lithuania was about three people in a gulag. They all turned in unison in their crammed bed just like the Occupation Museum said the prisoners did.

Amongst the many gorgeous churches in Lithuania's capital was a KGB Museum. The names of those "who died in interrogation" in this former KGB prison were carved on the outside walls. I tried differentiating the foreign names and wondered if that is what they will do to the outside walls of the Abu Ghraib prison someday. (But that is not in Eastern Europe.) Vilnius is the capital of Lithuania, and there I had *cepellinai* (dumplings made with potato dough; very Eastern European). By the time I reached Vilnius, I could tell the people around me were eating pig ears rather than clam strips and felt even more like I was far away from home. Outside the doors to the indoor market, an elderly man was selling a few mushrooms arranged on a hand towel that he had placed on the ground.

Still in Lithuania, I took a long walk in a National Park and my guide showed me the edible mushrooms. Interestingly, they were not as pretty as the poisonous ones. When I told people there that next to nobody in my hometown picked mushrooms growing in the woods, they seemed to find that incomprehensible. But then I had trouble comprehending much of their world too. I was telling my guide how I had enjoyed my time in Vilnius; he responded that Vilnius was now more like a European city rather than a Soviet town. When I asked why this was the case, the best explanation I received is that it had many new buildings. Another explanation about what made some parts of Eastern Europe more European than Soviet today was that under the Soviet Union, consumer goods from clothes to toys to candy bars had dull, drab colors. When the Soviet Union fell, one woman started collecting colorful candy wrappers.

She said she now wished she had saved some of the drab Soviet wrappers because that world has disappeared. I didn't notice many colorful buildings in Vilnius and I had not paid attention to the candy wrappers. Hmmm.

Warsaw is the largest city in Poland; it became the capital when Lithuania and Poland "unified" in 1569. During World War II, half of Warsaw's population perished and 85 percent of its buildings were destroyed. How they coped with that disappearance was to rebuild much of the city center using photographs of the buildings prior to World War II. The Royal Palace there is a UNESCO site that was rebuilt with money from Poles and Polish Americans. While the replicas of destroyed buildings almost denied the impact of World War II, the black and white photos at the City Museum stood witness to it. One photograph showed a crowded line-up of people hanging by nooses from the roof of a tall building and a marker explained these were resistance fighters hung by the Nazis upon their invasion. It is estimated that one-and-a-half to two million people in Warsaw were murdered (mostly Jews and some Gypsies, some Soviet prisoners of war, and the Polish resistance to the Nazi invasion). Another black and white photo showed a doctor who ran an orphanage in the Jewish ghetto; a sign explained how he had refused an opportunity to escape and instead chose to accompany the children of his orphanage to the gas chambers. Coping with a litany of past oppression was an unexpected but ongoing theme on this trip.

Polish author Czeslaw Milosz' *The Captive Mind* (1951) looks at the ways people cope with a repressive government. He notes people feel the need to conform so as not to arouse suspicion that they somehow might be an enemy of the State. A political cartoon in Warsaw succinctly summed up this sort of world when it showed a group of people on a picnic in the midst of nature whilst a "shepherd" sat on a nearby rock taking notes of the proceedings next to his sheep (people crouched on their hands and knees covered with sheep skins) who recorded the picnic with cameras and audio recorders. Milosz' book had a sculpture of a large, sideways head on its cover. In Krakow, I saw that head. It was possible to step inside the head and stick your head out of the eye socket. Krakow is referred to as the Boston of the East and featured numerous colleges and street performers. But Krakow is also just a few hours' drive from Oswiecim, the former Auschwitz prison complex set up by the Nazis during World War II. The Nazis persecuted the Communists in Poland. After the war, when the Communists came to power via the Soviet Union, the Polish parliament voted to preserve the Auschwitz prison camps as an historical monument.

The Nazis constructed this prison complex in 1940. There was a double wire fence around the Auschwitz camp and lookout towers were stationed at points along the fence. The guided tour of the prison complex yielded some reminders of the horror of war. The Nazis would kill a dozen prisoners if one prisoner escaped. Stakes rose up from the ground; nearby markers explained the prisoners were dangled from these stakes while tied up with their hands behind their backs. One group of cells was described as where prisoners were sent to starve to death. In frames on the walls were lines of photos of some prisoners. The information under each photo told of the prisoner's entry date and death date. Some died in days, some in weeks; one took 18 months. That sounded the worst. Information on prison life noted the prisoners received 1,500 calories a day, had access to toilets twice a day for 30 seconds at a time, had a change of underwear every three weeks, a shower once a month, and were punished for helping one another. The camps were set on a swamp so it was wet, and the winters were miserable. We saw a wall against which prisoners were executed; the Nazis had boarded the windows of the adjacent building so there wouldn't be any witnesses. But prisoners could still see the wall from an attic of another building. We saw cells where signs said prisoners were forced to stand through the night (four to a phone booth- sized stall) before going out for another day of hard labor. The prisoners were mustered for a count and then marched to work to an orchestra's music. Nazi propaganda photos showed an orchestra playing at Auschwitz.

Signs at Auschwitz said it was some British soldiers imprisoned there who were instrumental in getting the word out to the Red Cross that the Nazi's bathing facilities were gas chambers. We saw the gas chamber and were told they put pellets of Cyclon B into the underground room via the ceiling pipes, which caused people to die a very painful death from asphyxiation after 20 minutes. The Nazis would gun their trucks and motorcycles when stuffing the final screaming crowds inside the gas chambers, which were complete with shower nozzles. It seemed there had been definite efforts to keep "the final solution" a State secret. The corpses were shorn of hair and emptied of gold teeth before being triple-stacked onto coffin-like slots that were pushed into an oven. The burnt remains were used to fill in the swampy area around the camps or distributed for fertilizer.

The Nazis had transported Jews from all over Europe to Auschwitz and told them they were going to be resettled there. We saw train tickets that some had even purchased to get to the camps. Nazis placed the prisoners' belongings into warehouses to sort and ship the goods to Germany. The Jews could only take one piece of luggage to their new "homes" so many took precious items with them. There were rooms of luggage that were marked with the owner's surname, address and birth date; rooms of kitchen goods, rooms of shoes, rooms showing piles of human hair and rooms with stacks of eye glasses. Birkenau was the largest prison camp constructed in the Auschwitz complex. The retreating Nazis destroyed much of Birkenau, but American planes had taken aerial photos of the camps prior to their destruction. There were four gas chambers that held 2,000 people each. I saw the infamous track where the train pulled in and the platform on which Nazis determined those who would be sent for immediate extermination and those who would become laborers. People getting off the trains didn't know they were going to die. There was a black and white photo of three boys (about ages three, five, and seven) walking together with their arms around each other's shoulders looking hopeful though timid, and they were headed toward the gas chambers. They reminded me of my three nephews when they were younger; that is when the horror of the place finally got to me. That and the pair of tiny red ballet-style shoes with bows that were in the shoe pile in the room full of children's shoes. I think subsequent reflection proved more disturbing than the actual viewing. I returned to Krakow and procured some bison vodka (having a brand name pronounced *shoe-brew-fkah*) and blamed my inner discord on the full moon.

    Moving on to the Czech Republic, I switched from vodka to beer because a bottle of beer was less expensive than a bottle of water. In Prague, we were shown where the Protestants were killed and dismembered when the Hapsburgs imposed Catholicism upon the locals. The Czechs didn't seem to care for the Hapsburgs; our guide ruminated almost gleefully: "They started WWI and lost it!" We were shown a synagogue for which building construction was started in 1270 but not finished until the 1600s "because there was no rush." Hitler had even visited this synagogue as he planned to locate a museum about Jews there after he had eradicated them. The Czechs seemed to have a lot of experience being under siege. Just in the time I spent there, the *Prague Post* (in

English) included these two headlines: "Spying a thing of the Past? Not by a Longshot" and "Police with StB pasts to be vetted." I continued drinking beer and kept my head down. Continuing south to Cesky Krumlov, I toured the Eggenbert Brewery. The infrastructure of this working brewery was described as Soviet; it was not well maintained so that there was much rust and makeshift piping held together with duct tape. A worker using harsh chemicals chose to wear only one rubber glove. The fermentation vat was accessed by way of a narrow, circular stairway that stood at least 50 feet high but had no handrails. (Where was the local OSHA?) The Lithuanian's statement about Vilnius being more of a European city than a Soviet city "because it had newer buildings" was making more sense now.

I left the former Soviet bloc by way of Vienna, but it persisted in getting my attention. In Vienna, I viewed a photo exhibit of the 1956 Hungarian "uprising" when the Hungarian government had applied for NATO membership. At that time, the Soviet Union attacked and executed the president and many thousands of people. A sign explained that after World War II, the Soviet Union erected a barbed wire fence across the railroad track between Hungary and Austria, for safety no doubt, which was removed only in 1991. The security state continued to pursue me when my four-hour layover in London was just enough time to get through the security screening. We waited more than three hours to find out if anyone standing in our line had explosives. Posted warnings advised that physical assault on security personnel would incur criminal prosecution. To me, this indicated some level of understanding that the security measures were frustrating the travelers. In Boston, a guard dog on a leash sniffed the luggage. (My mind flashed to South America where I had been horrified at such police tactics at the airports.)

This particular journey is on my mind, because I still

can't seem to wrap my mind around it. I know it left me with a sense of ominous foreboding about homeland security paranoia. "He who forfeits liberty for security is doomed to lose both" is a quote often attributed to Benjamin Franklin. When I was seven years old, my neighbor raged against Vietnam War protesters saying, "Let them go to Russia if they don't like it here. You can't even raise your hand over there without permission unless you want to be shot!" I was in second grade and needing permission to raise your hand caused me to ponder that tirade a bit. I wouldn't want the US to become the Russia my neighbor had conjured. But I've always been a big subscriber to the slippery slope concept so maybe I'm overreacting. As my cousin said, you don't see people fighting to flee this country. That calmed me somewhat, but I'm still concerned. I grew up saying the Pledge of Allegiance almost every day. That's a lot of promising to stand up for liberty and justice for all.

Way out west felt far away. Maybe if I had worn boots...

20
Cow Talk

What do I remember about my four weeks in and around Colorado? On my return, at a stopover at the Newark airport, I recall seeing a man wearing a turban, women in Sunday clothes, and a lot fewer people wearing shorts. There were men with long overcoats, men wearing pastel T-shirts, and a man with long hair in a ponytail and a beard. I saw no cowboy boots and no men wearing hats. Wait…I take that back; there was one man in a lime green baseball cap. In addition to these people, there was a subway track outside the window. I recall thinking I was getting closer to home. I had been further away than I had planned.

Driving in from Pueblo, Colorado, going south toward Walsenburg, the scenery was dotted with low scrub bushes, telephone poles, and an occasional clump of tall grass. It was mostly empty land, but sometimes I saw clusters of cows: a multicolored group, a uniform group, or sometimes one or two individual cows. I soon gave up mooing as I drove by. They never moo back in that county. The highway speed is 75 miles per hour, and the roads are straight and fairly flat. Driving along, I was glad that I wasn't riding a horse on this endless prairie. Though I tried to fight it, Glen Campbell's *Rhinestone Cowboy* kept playing in my head. I drove over the Arkansas River; the land south of the Arkansas River used to be Mexico. I had never thought of Colorado being Mexican before. From the road, the river looked like it was being overcome by desert. Hmm…a Mexican desert.

In LaJunta in Otero County, the Mexican family restaurant was full of people speaking Spanish. That was different. Some meals became memorable. After ordering breakfast in that town, the waitress loudly snapped, "No meat?" I think she found that suspicious. Most of the next day (from 10:00 a.m. to 3:00 p.m.), I sat at a cattle auction. Cowboys, cattle…it seemed like something to do out West. The auctioneer would periodically remove the tissue from the microphone, wipe his mouth, place a new tissue over the microphone, and twist the ends around the microphone. He talked just as fast or even faster than they do in the Auctioneer song: *"What do you bid? What are you going to bid?"* It was all in English. He was at the center of a raised platform about six feet high in front of the ring where the cattle were shown.

The cattle ring was a round corral, which was entered through a revolving door. When an animal left the ring, a man next to the auctioneer opened the exit door, and the men in the ring hit the cattle until they walked into a hall where another man prodded them out of sight. The animals were encouraged into the ring with cattle prods (maybe to make them look lively), and then they were hit with plastic paddles held by metal rods so they would turn in circles. Two men were in the ring with paddles, and they jumped up onto the fence rails when the animals started to charge at them. This happened four times. One beautiful brown cow with horns trotted out and got up on her hind legs, resting her front hoofs on the corral fence while she looked over both exits to the ring. I liked her spirit. The animals were moved in and out quickly such that about two offers sold every five minutes. An animal seemed to be more in demand if it had no exposure to steroids and if its horns were removed. At the beginning, most animals were sold separately, but then it became more common to sell them in groups. After 1:00 p.m., there were a few groups with up to 30 cattle. There were calves, bulls, steer, heifers, and pregnant cows. Some animals had bloody noses. One group of cows was recalled when someone in the audience noted that one of the cows had a toe growing high on its leg. That group was split and bid separately. One calf had just been born that morning. When the asking price wasn't going anywhere, they split the calf and the mother for separate bids. One of the cowboys in the ring with the paddle carried the newborn calf out of the ring, but the guy on the outside stuck the calf with a cattle prod three times and then kicked it. I'm not sure what language it used, but that calf made me feel sad.

    The two cowboys maneuvering in the ring chewed tobacco, as did the man from Oklahoma two chairs to my right. He had arrived with a five-pound empty tin can into which he, in fact, spit. The people in the stands numbered about 50 with many coming in at around 11:00 a.m. While there were about two or three women and a couple of young children at various times, most of the people in attendance were old men wearing cowboy hats. White seemed to be the color of choice. Just about everyone but me was wearing blue jeans. Some wore cowboy boots. As far as I could tell, most of these old men were very subtle in their bidding. A few would raise their hand 12 inches upward, but most wouldn't even do that much. And each one seemed to do something a bit different. That is why the cowboys in the ring had such fixed stares as they scanned the crowd. To make extra sure I wasn't purchasing a cow, I stayed very still. My few serious itches managed to fade. Most of the animals were between 600 and 900 pounds. A number of them were about 1,025 pounds, and a few were around 2,000 pounds. I estimated the weight of each animal coming out and then checked my guess with the results printed on the electronic board above the auctioneer. That's what I did the whole time I sat so still on that hardwood seat. I'm not cut out for cattle auctions.

The man from Oklahoma told me they have cattle auctions in Massachusetts, and I said there were certainly a lot of cows in Massachusetts. But I thought to myself, they likely have cattle auctions in Oklahoma too, and I wouldn't be going to anymore anywhere. The cowboys in the ring seemed to hit the cows for no reason; above the cattle din I swear there was a mantra of DUMB COW being chanted. I liked the feisty ones that scared the men in the ring onto the fence. One cow wouldn't leave the ring; they didn't hit the ornery types. They tried to call it, lead it, and then finally they put a low-key bull in the ring. When the bull walked out, the cow followed. That bull must have been a real looker. Leaving there, my ears were ringing with the noise of cattle clamoring. A bumper sticker in the parking lot read: "I love animals. They're delicious." I'm glad I went to the cattle auction, but it felt good to move on.

At the Celestial Seasonings tea factory in Boulder, the sign stated that some hippies started the business in the 1970s and at that time, gathered herbs in the fields. Then, one sold his car to buy a sewing machine, and they sewed 8x4 inch canvas sacks to sell loose tea to health food stores. In the early days, the company t-shirt was tie-dyed and said: "Weeds for your needs." The tour was free; five others joined me on my tour. Our tickets were laminated tea box covers. The factory can produce two million boxes of tea each day. Kraft had bought the company, but its original owner bought it back in 1986. The factory was built in 1990. The company employs 200 people and about 20 of those worked with the machinery on the factory floor. Getting the tea into tea bags is done by robotics. We watched machines opening boxes and inserting wax liners. People, however, pack the boxes of tea into grocery store display boxes. We looked at a store merchandise display and were told that the ideal sales display is one that shows all of a company's products. They make 36 types of tea. Green tea and black tea are made from the same plant. The tour guide said people in Russia drink the most tea of any country. Celestial Seasonings' top customers are Canada, Japan, and New Zealand, respectively. Japan uses smaller boxes with 10 bags each because customers have less room to store surplus merchandise there. All other countries get regular sized boxes. We saw a map showing the different places in the world from which the company's herbs are bought. The peppermint tea was set apart in a room the size of a quadruple car garage. When the guide opened the door, my eyes felt an immediate sting. (I was glad I didn't have to work in that room.) At the beginning of the tour, a huge Sleepy Time Bear welcomed us to a display of entries to a teapot competition. One teapot was in the form of a raccoon, another teapot was a car with pursed lips for a spout. The teapots were dragons, houses and all sorts of creature teapots. No cows though.

Driving over the border into Utah, I saw prairie dogs along the side of the road. Those are the shy creatures you read about at zoos while looking at mounds of sand. Here, the prairie dogs were daring enough to dig on top of the sand. At one point, there was a morning bazaar full of them, and the scenery was brown sand full of mounds just like in the zoos. The next Utah treat was traversing past the canyons along the Westwater River with its fantastic scenery and Western Bluebirds. Then, I milled about Canyonlands National Park, awash in canyons mostly of reddish rock and very much the desert. I saw a few lizards. The sun was broiling me. I could almost hear my skin crackling. But it was awesome sitting on a ledge overlooking a huge red canyon contemplating the strange rock formations sprouting in no discernible pattern. No cows there either.

Back in Colorado, I kept driving. I have forgotten my destination now, but I was heading toward my reserved lodging and driving on a narrow road leading high up into the mountains. Elk were everywhere. After some hours into my ascent, it started to snow. In minutes, it seemed, I found myself driving through two feet of snow. Too close to my destination to turn around now, I plowed on until I reached the roadblocks and the signs saying, Road Closed. In disbelief, I managed to turn around and continue plowing through the blinding snow, somehow staying on the road. It was late afternoon when I pulled into the small town of Idaho Springs. Still stricken, I pulled over at the only lodging to be seen. The woman at the desk didn't want my business because a group of actors was onsite practicing for a play or some such thing. I pressed on. She showed me her only vacancy, a small room with an unmade bed and gum wrappers on the floor. I insisted it would suffice. To my relief, she let me have the room. The next morning, I set out to explore my unexpected landing place.

The notorious gunslinger Doc Holliday reportedly stayed there. A sign said he had come for a summer to bathe in "the waters of Idaho Springs" hoping for a cure for tuberculosis. Charlie Taylor's waterwheel was still standing; he had built it in 1893 to power the stamp mill at his gold mine operation. With all the people who had come there looking to be cured through bathing, I wondered how much credence had been given to Mr. Taylor's crediting his good health to his avoidance of bathing. To give his method its full due, he combined that with not kissing women. Did he kiss men? Was it that kissing women would necessitate bathing? Reading about Mr. Taylor reminded me of the Delta town museum's collection of curious signs, all advising to "Spit at Home." In the 1890s, that town had outlawed spitting in public. Men would spit in public places, and the women's long dresses would drag on the ground such that the spit was brought into the home. This spread tuberculosis and led to the local ordinance that prohibited spitting in public. (Posting "Spit at Home" signs at the cattle auctions

might be a good idea.) I walked over to see the hot mineral springs that had lured Doc Holliday and so many others. The sign said the waters were residual fluids from the process of mineralization that produced gold.

All of this was further explained at the Western Museum of Mining and Industry, but it didn't interest me as much as the social dimension of mining. In the 1880s, most miners were Welsh or Irish and animosity between the two groups ran high. By the 1890s, these groups had joined ranks to fight the Italians and the Swedes. The Chinese and Native Americans were the most shunned in mine work, but they were nevertheless working some of the plum jobs. The men who set the dynamite were called powder monkeys. Another nine men would gather on a tiny platform and free fall down the shaft to reach their mining destination. The muckers shoveled 16 tons of rock per 10-hour shift. The shaft wheel operator operated the "elevator" and could apply the brakes somewhat for the descent. The drillers pounded a three-foot rod into stone for the dynamite, and if they didn't turn the rod between poundings, it would get stuck in the rock. Many of these workers had come in search of gold. The museum sign said some Colorado gold seekers didn't know where Colorado was until they got there; many didn't know much about prospecting, and it was said that some even decided where to dig by following the lead of their mule when it was inclined to go toward a particular rock. There was a model showing the stamp that crushed the rock and pushed the crushed rock (including gold) onto the conveyor belts that were covered with mercury. The gold stuck to the mercury and then it was scraped off. So the mad hatters were in the company of the mad miners. The gist of the museum is that mining is necessary and that gold seekers settled the West in a way that probably wouldn't have happened absent a glut of frenzied people from all over the world who traveled to the Western states to become millionaires overnight. That is why there were so many desperate folks eager to work in the harsh mining camps.

Back in the capital city of Denver at the Colorado State Museum, I saw a display on artwork depicting Cheyenne Dog Soldiers. If three arrows missed the hero in battle, the picture depicted all three in the air. One warrior in each party wore a long sash and would dismount his horse, put one end of the sash over his neck and attach the other end of the sash onto a stake in the ground; this was to show that he would fight to the death. (By then, I had deleted "miner" and "dog soldier" from my list of possible careers.) Still in Denver, I took a tour of the United States Mint, where I saw pennies pouring in a heap into a large vat and piles of quarter shapes waiting to be imprinted. While it was good to see where it all happens, I wouldn't exactly call Denver a happening place. Yet, notably, I had my first taste of buffalo meat there, and the New Yorkers who had moved there seemed very friendly. They were so fun and gracious, I even paid their bar bill, no small bill. It can pay to be good to solo travelers.

I moved on and visited Mesa Verde National Park. Mesa Verde has a large canyon rim around deep crevices that form narrow valleys. They say there was a thriving civilization there from the 700s to 1200s. The inhabitants farmed on the tops of the rim and hunted in the forested valleys below. (They must have been in good physical shape.) At Mesa Verde, I hiked the Petroglyph Trail, a three-mile loop. The trail attempted to share the natural environment of the Mesa Verde and instruct about how it was used by the early people residing there. I walked narrow passages between tall rock walls and emerged to awesome views of the canyon. When I finally reached the petroglyphs at the end of the trail, I was relieved. I had been beginning to worry there may be none despite the name Petroglyph Trail. A petroglyph is an image carved into the face of a rock. This trail featured a cluster of clearly discernible figures carved onto the rock above a narrow path. I knew I would not have stood on the open ledge to chip the design into the sandstone until the interior color of the rock showed through. So seeing any carved images was impressive to me. When I reached the petroglyph, I caught up with two women (ages 77 and 80) from California. I was glad I met with them because about 50 feet further up the trail, we got to climb around the side of a ledge using hand holds and toe holds. This was fairly easy, but I would have been nervous going over that exposed ledge without them. It was somehow comforting to know that if I slipped, someone was there to report my fall. After that stretch, we were rewarded with the best view of the surrounding canyon and its colorful wildflowers.

Crossing over to Wyoming, I visited the museum in Jackson Hole. There it told how Wyoming has a long history of women in politics. Wyoming had the first female governor in the US. In 1920, all the city officials elected in Jackson were female, and I picked up a postcard with their photograph. The museum noted that Mr. John Coulter, in 1807, had been the first white man to enter Yellowstone National Park. (There are lots there now). Wyoming license plates have a cowboy motif. At hootenannies (musical open-microphone nights), people are respectfully attentive to the entertainment. I was impressed.

It seemed to storm from two o'clock to three o'clock like clockwork. They say it is best to keep moving along the trail in a thunder and lightning storm rather than stop under a rock for shelter. A long and thick flash of lightning in a dark cloud looked like it had cut a slit in the mountain. I had read a journal by a woman who had homesteaded in Wyoming and loved it so I looked upon the trails and the lightning with borrowed fondness. The Wyoming locals I met were mostly people who had moved there from other states. One woman told me how she and her husband had moved from Colorado to raise their family in Wyoming. The people were trustworthy, it seemed; she felt she could let her children play outside there without fearing for their safety. She said, "Good people live in Wyoming." I didn't ask if that was because they are white people who speak English. Why people confide these sorts of impressions to me has always been puzzling. But the barbecue options were straightforward. I liked Wyoming a lot too.

After driving through the beautiful, green Grand Tetons, I reached Yellowstone National Park. I entered the south entrance through roads plowed in the snow. The snow had been plowed so that the road was lined with jagged, five-foot high snow banks, which looked like giant white Arabian pointed slippers lined up along the roadside. Beyond the snow, I could see spruce trees all around. Then, the snow tapered off and many dead standing trees appeared. The trees died when the boiling waters flooded them, and the remaining trunks act like wicks drawing the water and minerals from the ground. The scenery changed again so that I returned to a world of green, with a rolling river and spruce trees in front of mountains where bald eagles soared overhead and a bunch of buffalo ambled in the forefront.

The roaming buffalo proved popular with the tourists. Talk of not re-introducing wolves to protect the buffalo population was in the news. As I drove by, one buffalo became irritated and kicked its back legs at the sky. I was surprised to see such limber action, as I had mostly seen buffalo standing stone still in zoos. They say buffalo average 2,000 pounds and can run 35 miles per hour. Given that, I turned back when a buffalo, undaunted even by my rendition of *We All Live in a Yellow Submarine*, insisted on blocking my path. The buffalo didn't seem to care that I had walked four miles to breakfast at the upcoming waterfall. Bring in the wolves, say I.

At the site of the geyser Old Faithful, the scenery took a dramatic turn to mostly grey. I walked the boardwalk trail among the geysers, sinkholes, mud flats, and fumaroles. The sign said these features were present because the earth's core was closer to the earth's surface there. The steam had a sauna feel, and the constant smell of rotten boiled eggs made me see fried eggs in many of the bubbling pools and scrambled eggs in the rough clay-like terrain. There was a brief interlude of color at Inspiration Point, a ledge overlooking colorful canyon walls, and a waterfall that flowed at one end of the canyon. It looked as if "terraces" of oil paints had fallen whilst a sloppy giant was painting a picture. No buffalo there. Did the giant painter scare them off? Next, I walked about the Norris Geyser Basin, and the world was back to shades of grey. A decomposing buffalo carcass rested on grounds that looked like an off-white ceramic planet with craters (like those on the moon). The sound was the geyser's most marked feature. It had the sound of a slow coffeepot perk or a slow pressure cooker noise. I imagined an underground factory at work. One rock was surrounded by bubbling mud. Thunder in the distance added a whole new dimension. Smoke was puffing out of the craters. I decided the smoke was from the water pipes smoked by genies who were quietly biding their time in this portal to another world. That explained all the pointed slippers by the side of the road. I think the genies were sneering at me because I was still thinking about the cows.

I enjoyed my time in the West. I had no appointments to keep so I stopped everywhere from scenic small towns such as Delta and Paonia to tourist towns such as Grand Junction and Jackson. Colorado Springs had mountain scenery of beautiful red rock, a laid-back bookstore restaurant, and a college radio station that rocked. I had a flaming fajita in the Town of Golden, where I watched slides of Buffalo Bill who toured with

Annie Oakley. By the Rocky Mountains, I meditated near a pond with a bullfrog chorus chanting some unintelligible mantra. I saw a foot pedal dentist drill, which reminded me of the Western flick where Don Knotts played a dentist who had "Gone West." I rode through the Colorado Monument with its huge bottles of rock. I studied water sprinklers set on horizontal poles held up by wooden wagon wheels. Mostly, I watched waterfalls and ordered ice cream sodas. I think this trip accounts for my Far Side mug with the cow family driving their car on roads winding through pastures where the people roam. The calf in the back seat yells *yakkety yak* to the people they drive by.

Caving opened my eyes about what I wasn't seeing on the surface.

21
Trolls, Dwarves and the Human Race

While driving with my nephew, he pointed at the sink holes along the side of the road and remarked how that looked like a good spot for spelunking. After I learned that verb meant crawling around in underground caves, I felt a great anxiety come upon me. It happened time and again until I realized I might have a phobia. I had climbed around rock caverns all through my childhood, but the thought of being completely underground was unsettling. So what else was there to do but face it head on? I signed up for a weekend of underground exploration. Caving took preparation. First, I obtained a pair of gardening gloves. Then, I had to procure some sort of knee protection. None felt comfortable. I settled for children's kneepads to which I added extra band material. I found a children's book on caves at the library; it was just my speed. And, I gathered together a collection of flashlights and put a candle and some matches in a tin box. The day after my return, I recorded using Ben-gay lotion for aches and pains and wearing black nylons and a long black skirt to cover my blotched and bumped legs. Such is the life of a cave explorer.

"Caving is an exciting (and very dirty) sport of discovery. We will be exploring two caves in eastern New York State. We can expect to spend at least a few hours underground in each cave exploring large tunnels, small squeeze holes and hidden passages. At times we will be walking upright, other times we'll be bent over, sometimes we'll be crawling, and other times we'll be wiggling on our stomachs. We can expect to get pretty dirty and we will sometimes be in waist-high water. Fortunately, the temperature in a cave remains consistent year round and it will be around fifty degrees or warmer inside the caves regardless of how cold it is outside." So goes the introductory note on the cover sheet to my packing list. Intriguing? Let the play begin.

    I made it to the departure point on time. The bus was still in the parking lot. I think I was excited. I know I signed the release before reading it; so unlike me. I didn't even pretend to read it. Then after signing it, I read it. Ten of us started off in a painted-over school bus for Schoharie, New York. There were nine of us who had signed on for this caving trip: two teenagers, two in their twenties, me, and the rest in their forties. Three of us were female. One person was from France and one was from Ohio and the rest of us were from Massachusetts and New Hampshire; it was a good mix. The guide and bus driver, Larry, offered us his selection of caving magazines for the ride. He explained that the better caves were west of the Connecticut River and were of limestone. The caves to the east of the river are generally from fault lines in the earth. Anyway...we rode on dark roads off Route 88 in New York. We took some narrow paved roads onto a dirt road and parked in what looked like the middle of the woods. We put up our tents and walked to the nearby cave. It was down a hill with a walk-in entrance. It had a cellar feel to it, and I could see that to go past the entrance, we would have to walk through water. A few bats flew out of the cave while we were inspecting the entrance. That was it. We all knew we would be upset if we didn't get to see a bat on the next day's walkabout in the cave.

    Breakfast was delicious but how Larry made the coffee was unique. Boil water, put in coffee, stir and set. Bring to a boil, cover, then wind your arm in a wide circle while holding the pot. No need for filters or strainers.

Grounds sink to the bottom of the pot. I'll concentrate on anything not to let myself get caught in my fear about going WAY underground and not to think too much about the bats and white crayfish and the smell of bat excrement that the children's book mentioned. I thought everybody else seemed curious and ready for adventure, so I was determined not to reveal any paranoia.

We dressed for caving. We taped our lights onto our helmets and adjusted the helmet with a knob to secure it firmly on our heads. We went in. The water felt the coldest when it reached my kneecaps or my waist. The walls were covered with wet mud. I stepped slowly through the water because I couldn't see the bottom. Walls sometimes had bubbly surfaces. We passed a wrought iron gate with a decorative spider on it! The guide explained that this cave was opened as a tourist attraction for one day (to enable the owner to use it as a tax shelter). We were given maps of the cave and learned 0/3 means zero feet of air and three feet of water at that point in the cave. We saw stalactites and drapes (rock in the form of folding drapery). I had taken two right-handed gloves so I kept them in my pocket and touched cold, muddy walls. The hanging bats were about six feet higher on the walls than where my hands pressed so that was fine. At one point, we saw a group of 12 bats hanging together. They were medium brown and furry and each was about 4x4 inches. The bats tried to ignore us, but sometimes one would open its eyes after 10 flashlight beams were directed on it. The further we went, the more it smelled like ammonia, that was the bat *guano* (bat dung). We successfully completed tricky climbs around corners on slippery smooth rock, and we went stemming. Stemming is straddling water below by using your feet, elbows, and hands to move along tunnel walls over the water. Sometimes, it would feel like doing the splits. Every once in a while you could hear someone fall in.

Somehow, I didn't. The cave was a half-mile deep, and we walked in 2,000 feet to the end. Then we turned back. Two of my three flashlights failed: it was the batteries on the first and the bulb on the second. The third flashlight saw me through so I didn't have to use my candle. When you turn your light off in a cave, it is completely black such that you can't even see your hand pass before your eyes. I guessed that must be what blindness is like. We slowly walked back to the entrance while admiring the cave's mysterious ins and outs. I recall feeling a greater respect for the dark.

We lunched in the forest. Rain came. Then we took the bus to the NSS (National Speleology Society) bookstore. There the guide picked up our permit to enter the cave we had just explored that morning. Alas, the bookstore was closed. We drove to the general store, and the one person who had brought a camera purchased film. The rain stopped, and we walked through the woods along a path with gorgeous wild flowers to Knox Cave's sink hole. Down a steep hill was a huge hole; the thought of descending into that hole was scary. The guide advised that the next day's cave had a sinkhole entrance. The NSS is secretive as to the whereabouts of its caves and when we saw three cavers rappel up from Knox Cave, they looked annoyed that we had seen them exit.

Back at camp around 6:00 p.m., we decided to go swimming. We walked down a long series of steep hills and then crossed a bridge near a farm with goats and cats and cows and chickens wandering around. Under the bridge and around the bend was a rocky beach with many of the stones showing clear fossil imprints of shells and such. The creek was deep and clear and refreshing. On the way back to camp after skimming lots of stones, I stopped to view the rock collection displayed in and about a yard along the way; rock was the weekend theme. Trudging up that series of hills to camp was a humbling experience. The youngest among us had brought fire starters so we were able to get the wet wood to burn to a huge, high fire. We toasted marshmallows.

Next morning, we packed up camp. My suitcase was almost empty. My wet, muddy clothes from caving at Schoharie were in a plastic trash bag. My caving clothes for the day were set out and waiting on the bus, and I was wearing my dry camp clothes. We lit a fire and ate our breakfast with a gorgeous view of rolling hills and hints of the fantastic foliage to come. It was a half-hour bus ride to this day's cave in Clarksville. The cave had a private owner who ran the nearby diner, not the NSS. We parked in an elevated lot above and in back of the owner's diner. As we walked into the woods, Larry told us that a counterfeiting operation had once used this next cave.

We walked to a 20x20 foot dip in the forest. In this dip, was a small (about 3x3 foot) sink hole. There was the option to go in headfirst. We all went in feet first, about five feet down and headed north toward the Lake Room. I saw no bats but did see bat droppings. We went under and under, and then went through low tunnels. Stalactites thrust down from ceilings, making them seem even lower. We crawled quite a bit, which was fine because the rocks were wet and slippery under foot. I wore gloves for this cave, thank goodness. We climbed around smooth and slippery and slanted rock to the narrow Twinkle Room, where we saw the beginning of a small tunnel called Polly Avenue. A caver had been stuck in Polly Avenue for six days. We peered into the tunnel and were told she had been stuck some 40 feet beyond the entrance. I hoped she had managed to make herself unconscious. We climbed into the waist high water in the Lake Room and then by semi-crawling went through a low and watery but wide winding tunnel with lots of stalactites. This was an exhausting feat, but at the same time I discovered an awesome route for toy Viking boats.

Fascinating—-like a land where trolls might live. Larry, the guide, was more geared toward exploring the possible than considering the most prudent thing to do. That was good for me, as I'm an ever- timid soul. I followed him into a very tight tunnel. When he said we had gone far enough, I said we needed to push in further so others could appreciate the sensation. We did and it got much tighter. Getting out, I asked if I could turn around (asking for suggestions not possibilities) and of course he said yes (responding to a question about the possibility). I admit I was getting awfully anxious, and I almost lost my balance in the maneuver. (I remember thinking about Houdini saying that you need to relax to get out of tight places.) Finally, I did back out of this tight low crouch and made haste to get out of the constricting tunnel.

We left the cave for lunch in the forest. I was a bit frazzled. My wet clothes were feeling chilly. Soon it was time to return to our cave exploration, however. We were heading south this time. Feet first into the sinkhole, and then I raised myself upward diagonally head first through a small opening. Diagonals mixed with verticals made for a bizarre route that sometimes led upward and sometimes downward. The helmet's visor stopped my vision at horizontal so I had to turn my head to look for the next vertical and/or diagonal opening. The nerve-wracking part was seeing an apparent blockage in the route before realizing I needed to tilt my head to the side to look around for the next opening. Moving along the low passages was the least pleasant part of the exploration. Pushing myself along on my stomach, I would turn my head to look up and see what looked to be room enough to crawl on my knees rather than slither on my stomach. While the space around my helmet seemed to have sufficient height to let me get up on my knees, that was only true for the space in front of me because the stalactites over my trunk would keep me flat on the ground if I tried to get up on my knees. But still, I would try to raise myself onto my knees and feel something hard over my back preventing me from rising. I couldn't see what it was because of the helmet and limited tunnel space. When my back was held down, my mind wasn't immediately figuring out why. My first thought was goblins. Truly, my first impression was consternation, but we must find something tangible to hold onto. After a while, I came around to the reality that I could move easily by getting grips in the dirt with my hands and feet and pushing myself along. So why try to crawl? I got through the low tunnels and slid down a smooth 20-foot slide of rock into a foot of water. Then the opening big enough for me turned direction and led to high but narrow walkways. I tramped in and around rocks until the pièce de résistance appeared...a rock overhang obstructing the path that required taking a long breath, jumping in and swimming under water for a distance of 8 feet to clear the overhang and continue on the path. I estimated it was about 0/5 in cave notation. Even though I'm a strong swimmer, it gave me pause because I knew the directions in cave routes could switchback rapidly. As it turned out, it was a wide curve and I emerged on the other side with enough open space over the water to breath air. Dripping wet in my caving gear, I walked out of the cave by way of a six-foot high tunnel, a cylinder of sunshine. That sun looked good.

    We walked back to the bus and posed for a group photo. After changing into dry clothes, we walked over to look at the Thook entrance: a long, narrow, and very steep cave entrance into which one would need to rappel. The group sat for some time to discuss our impressions. One said he just kept hoping someone had not blocked the exit while we were below ground. I still remember thinking how glad I was I had not even considered that possibility while I was diving downward through the angular tube section. We headed back on the bus.

Upon arriving at my parents' house for a gathering, I was very stiff. My mother said I looked exhausted. I had been there and back. Days later, I was still in somber meditation. Do goblins live somewhere at the end of those tunnels? Were there dwarves watching my every move underground? If you fall asleep in a cave, do the trolls cart you away? Because of this adventure or maybe these questions, I decided to go to Carlsbad Caverns in New Mexico.

A month later, I was at the Blue Corn Cafe in Santa Fe waiting for soup and cheese enchiladas with Christmas chilies (red and green). It was a whole new cuisine for me, because New England didn't have much of that until the 1990s. My city walking tour included three cathedrals: one Romanesque built by a French friar, one gothic built by the Spaniards, and one adobe built by the Pueblo Indians. Santa Fe was very foreign looking to me, and it was with some regret that I left the tall, colorful forms with the horned heads standing outside the art galleries. I drove south to Roswell on Route 285, through a huge void of flat land with sparse, low, brown grass. It was like driving down the middle of an ever-constant pancake. It was even rare to see another car, and there were no streetlights and hardly a gas station but just a stretch of void like in a Star Trek voyage. In fact, there was nothing but empty, flat, brown scrub fields from 30 miles south of Santa Fe all the way to Vaughn. Visions of a blowout haunted me even while singing my torch songs, which are usually able to block out all unsettling visions. It grew more surreal when I ran over a large white jackrabbit. It looked like a white rabbit in the middle of the road but it couldn't have been because its ears reached over the hood of my car. When I arrived at the hotel after that 4-hour drive, I told the desk clerk I had run over something that looked like a white rabbit but was much bigger. He just said: "Those jackrabbits get pretty big." I was sure my photo was on the wall of every rabbit-hole post office by now. I was going too fast to stop, and the white creature with the long, tall ears kept stepping from side to side rather than getting out of the road. I just felt awful about it.

The next day, I drove to Slaughter Canyon Cave, south of Carlsbad on the Texas border. The mile-long hike to Slaughter Canyon Cave was an easy trek. The cave passages were easy but sometimes slippery. We used a rope to maneuver over the slippery slopes. Many bats with long and narrow wings hung from the walls. I saw a white cricket; a featured creature in the children's library book on caving. Some spaces were huge; one had a column 90 feet high. A rock formation about 50 feet tall looked just like the head of Darth Vader. Looking into passages behind these huge rock formations, I could make out lots of long stalactites creating a curvy obstacle course. I suspected that is where the trolls hang out. In spite of my trepidation, I managed to come away with a Certificate of Bravery from the American International Rattlesnake Museum later in the trip.

I arrived at Carlsbad Caverns the night after the fruit bats flew to Mexico for the winter. At dusk, I waited with a crowd of people at the cave entrance (90 feet wide and 40 feet high) but no bats came out. The ranger talked to us a bit to fill the void of no bat stampede coming from the caves. At one point, I remember him saying, "We're related in a way; his father and my father were both fathers." More successfully, I toured Carlsbad Caverns the next day from 8:30 a.m. to 3:30 p.m. There was a guided tour of the King's Room, the Queen's Room, and the Papoose Room. Then I descended alone into the cave through its surface entrance. I sensed magical worlds in that cave. Dwarves of stone remained still whilst they sensed the human's observation. Miniature kingdoms shrouded themselves so that they looked like drip sand castles. Scuba diving sites with mostly algae and sponges about a coral reef seemed to have turned to stone. More provocative than my places of contemplation at home, I tried to soak up the sensations.

A ranger-guided tour of the lower cave lasted for two and a half hours. Rangers provided helmets with lights attached, and luckily I had a pair of torn gloves in the car. We descended three ladders and saw lots of water; thus, we knew the cave formations were still very active. There were some good examples of sideways growths (helictites). A scientist showed us where he was monitoring drips to learn more about how long it takes water to seep underground. His aim was to address concerns that the Southwest is pumping water from the earth faster than it can replenish itself. Carlsbad Caverns were formed by the percolating ground waters in a limestone fossil reef some three to five million years ago. We were about 1,840 feet underground. Wow.

Leaving Carlsbad, I went to Albuquerque. I walked around the Old Town Section and purchased some gifts at the souvenir shops. At one jewelry shop, I talked a bit with the people working the counter. They said that everyone comes to New Mexico to see the Pueblos, the traditional habitats of Pueblo Indians. I explained how I had just come to see Carlsbad Caverns. They convinced me I might be missing out so I stopped in at the Indian Pueblo Cultural Center. Once there, I watched a video about an Indian artist who grinds different rocks to get various paint colors to use in painting memories of pueblo life. I bought a bunch of chili peppers on a string, but when I asked about them, I was told chili peppers were brought there by the Spanish rather than being part of the traditional Pueblo fare. After studying the Pueblo Cultural Center's exhibits, I decided I would visit the Acoma Pueblo the next day before heading home. That evening a luminous full moon shone over the mountaintops as I drove to the University of New Mexico. The university's art museum displayed old photos from 1880 to 1910 including a life-sized portrait of a pueblo chief in traditional costume. The best exhibit was "The attack of the Scorpions," a clay rendering of an amphitheater filled with one inch people being invaded by black scorpions of about four inches in length. The parking lot attendant steered me to a great college hangout with cool and colorful paintings of animals in drag. The recommended *posale* (chili soup with pork and corn) was delicious.

First thing in the morning, I drove to Acoma and visited Sky City, a well-established pueblo when Coronado reached New Mexico in 1540. I got there in time to jump on the bus for the first morning tour. A huge rock formation about 500 feet in length that looked like a stegosaurus sat in the valley where we boarded the bus. It gave me chills just looking at it being the dinosaur buff that I am. We were cautioned not to photograph the rock. (Would a photo animate the stegosaurus?) The bus ride took us up a winding road, 357 feet to the village on top of the mountain. There was a mission in the village that was built by Indians enslaved by Spanish friars. The guide said the second bell in the tower was exchanged for eight Indian children sold as slaves in Mexico. With that sort of information being in the script, you would think they would have mentioned the Pueblo Revolts but I think those weren't until the 1600s. As the Spanish had ultimately returned, I didn't feel comfortable raising the topic. I remember climbing down the ladder into the hollow *kiva* (a men's place for ceremonies), a room below the ground surface, and being pleased at how well it fit with the caving theme of my trip.

After the guided tour, we were given the option to walk down the mountain on the traditional path or take the bus back to the bottom. I opted to walk and was taken aback to find that it was a steep pathway of rock. In Massachusetts, anything with a reasonable amount of challenge for the public would not be an option thanks to liability fears. Here, there were hand holes and smooth rock surfaces, and I still can't believe anyone accomplished this hike balancing a water container on his or her head. (If I fell, how long before I would be found?) The walk down did let you admire, at your leisure, the imposing rock formations in the valley. Once at the bottom, I walked to the Visitor Center, where I had Acoma's traditional fried bread (light fried dough served with a container of honey) and where I toured a small museum. Then, as I was leaving, I stopped at some outdoor tables where people were selling ceramics. I bought a wedding vase for my cousin's wedding anniversary gift. It was a black and white vase with a handle on either side. The guide had told us that if a couple got divorced, they pulled on the vase handles (like pulling on a turkey wishbone) and the one who pulled the bigger piece of the vase got the marriage property. I liked that idea. In my short time in New Mexico I found myself pondering the veracity of such fanciful suggestions. (Were the people so subtle or was I so overtired?)

While I took this extension trip to deal with my caving anxiety by facing caves head-on, I came away with much more. This trip remains on my mind because for most of my time in New Mexico on the less-treaded paths, I was referred to as "the white woman." I recall feeling like an inadequate standard-bearer and thinking it just wasn't fair that a whole race should be marked with my shortcomings. Looking back, I think for a mill town girl from New England, where there is no such thing as a "white" woman, it was an educational experience. Where I'm from, you might be English or French or Italian or German or Polish or even some combination, but you are never just white. Maybe I need to get out more.

www.ingramcontent.com/pod-product-compliance
Lightning Source LLC
Chambersburg PA
CBHW071814080526
44589CB00012B/792